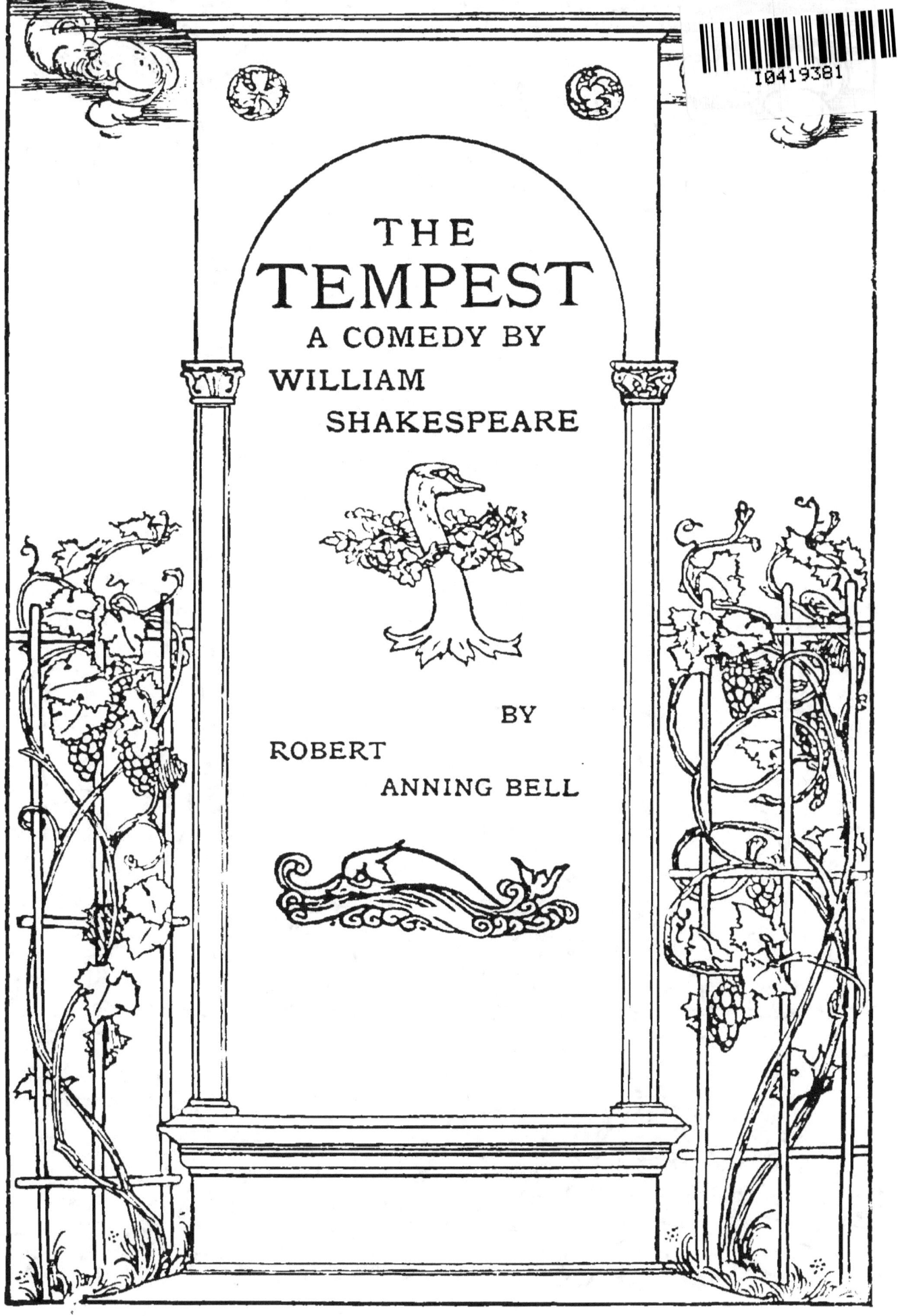

THE TEMPEST

A COMEDY BY
WILLIAM SHAKESPEARE

BY
ROBERT ANNING BELL

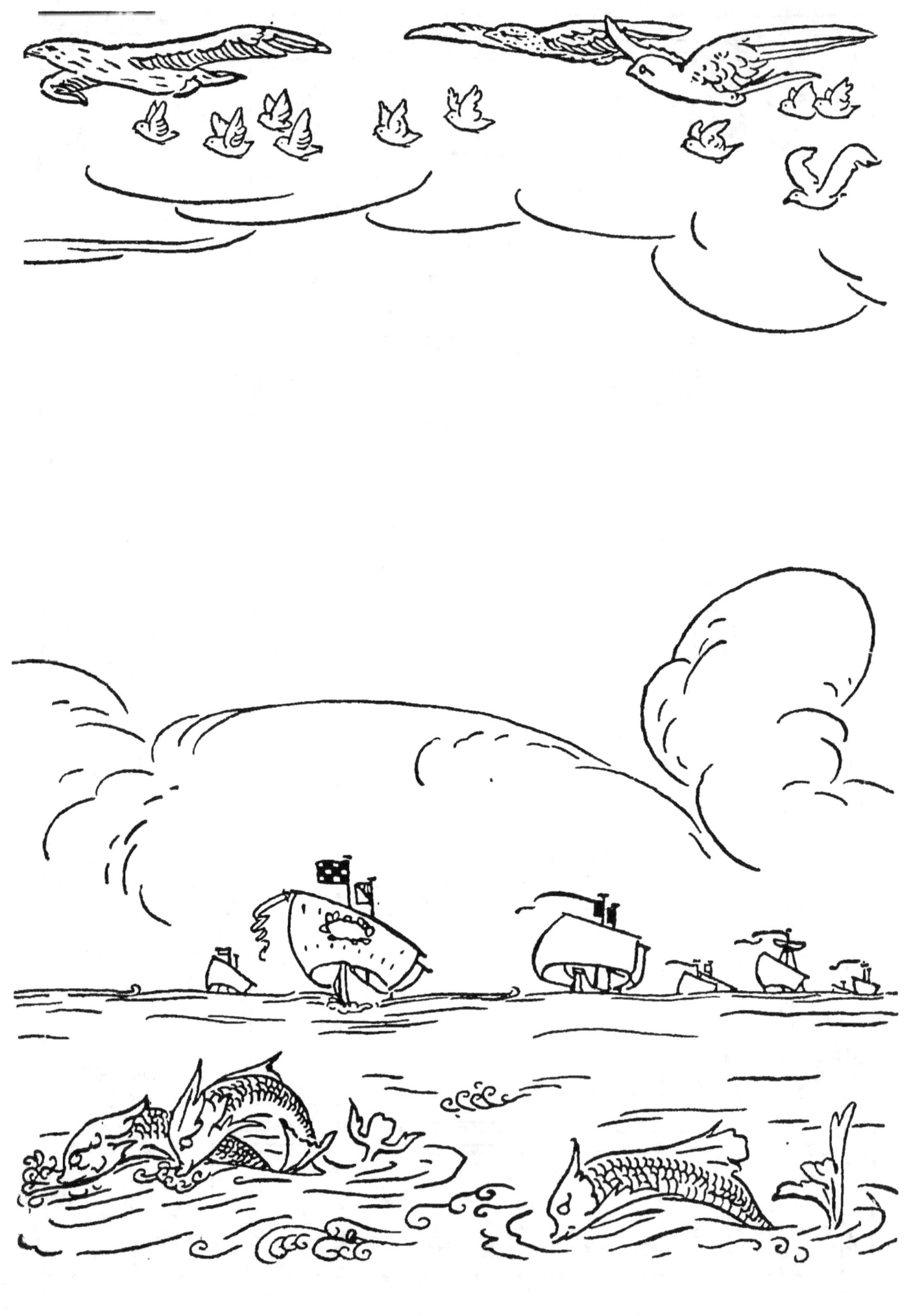

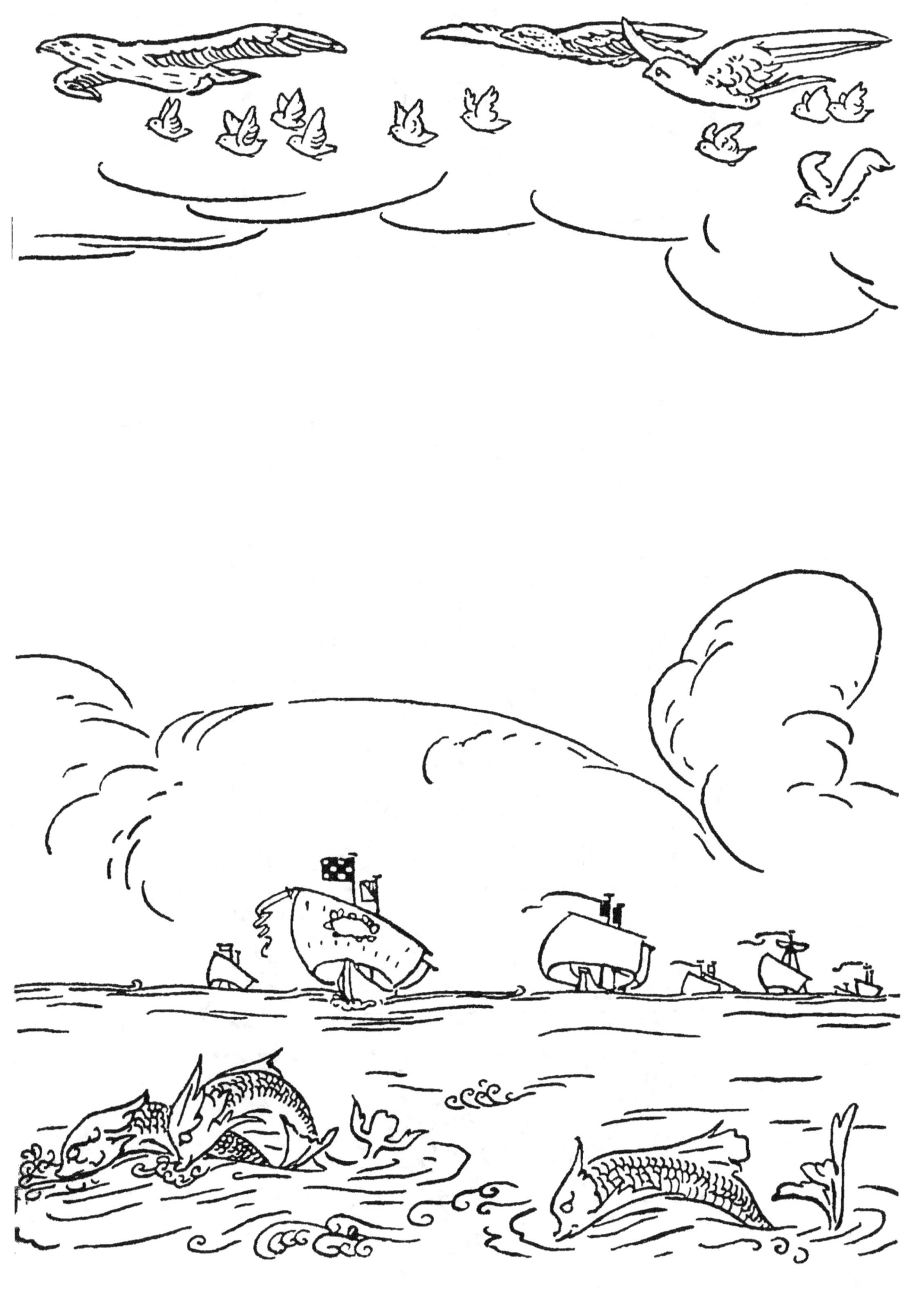

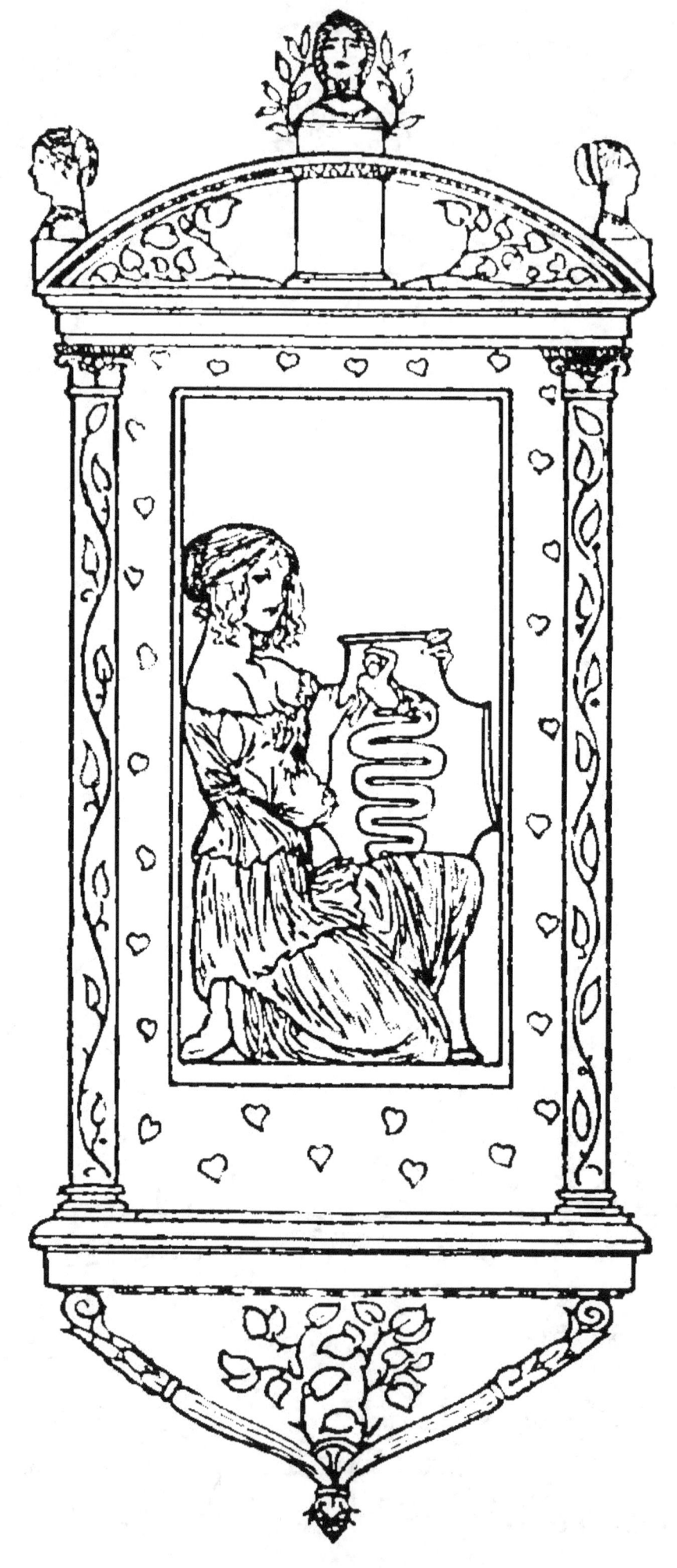

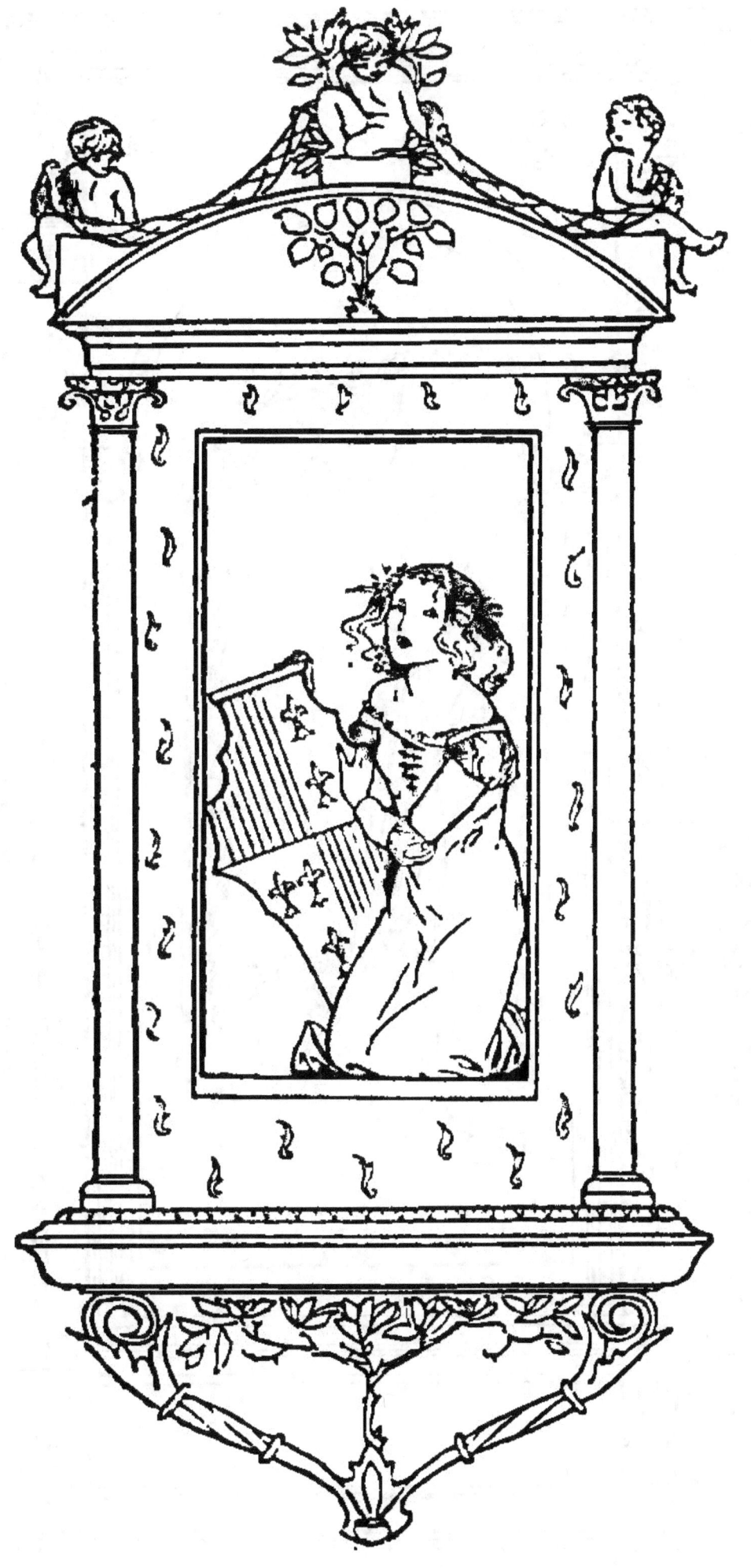

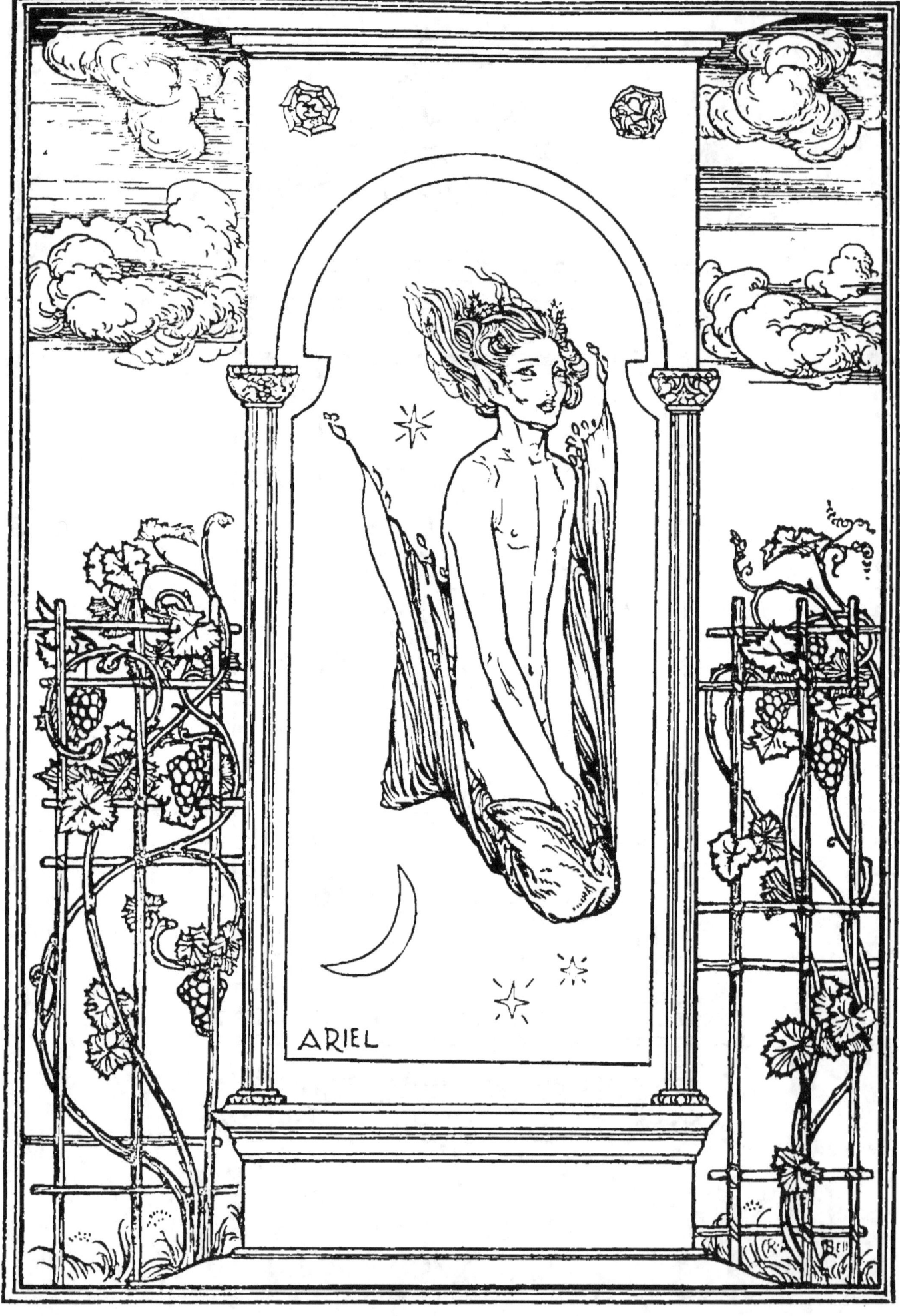

ARIEL

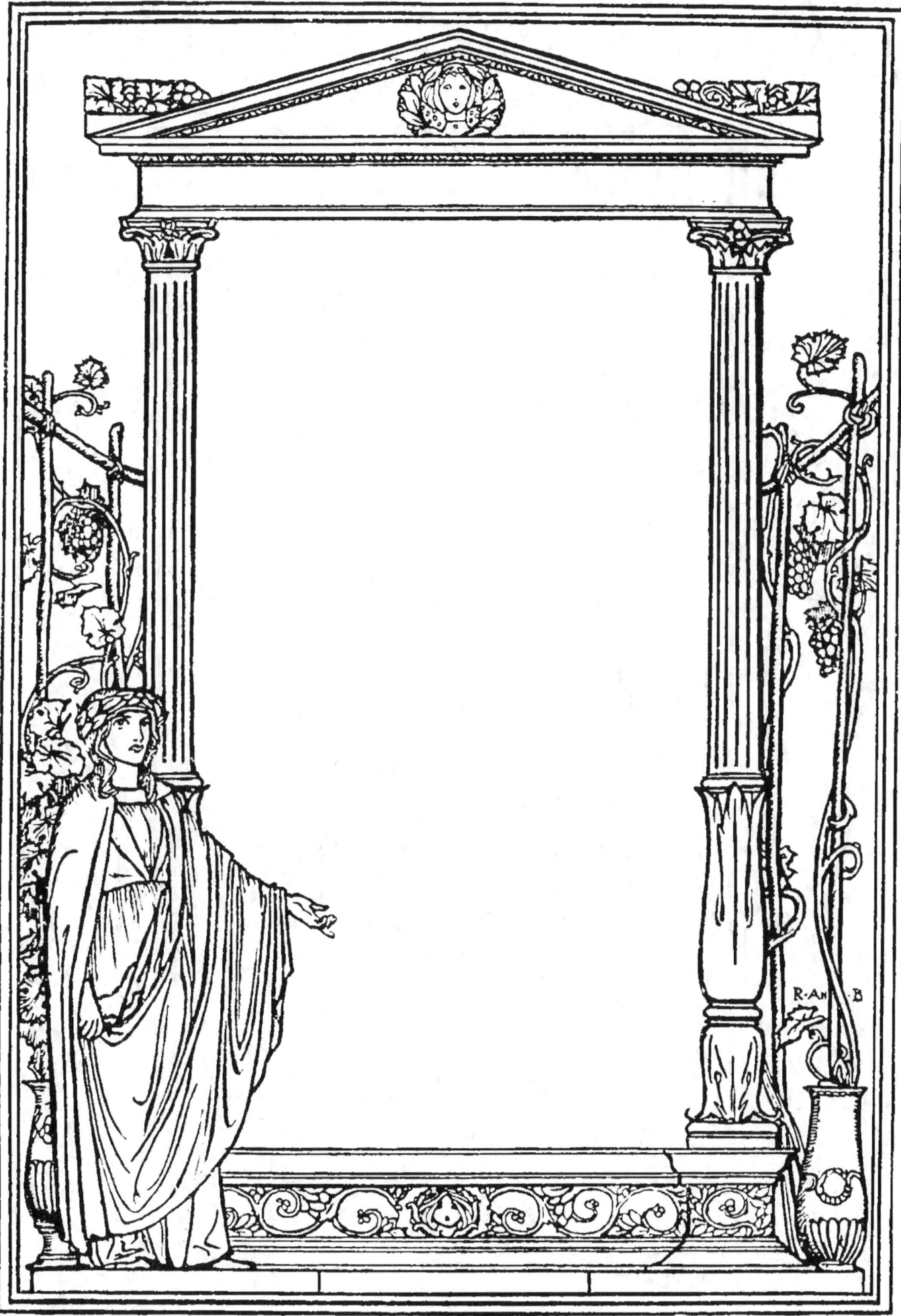

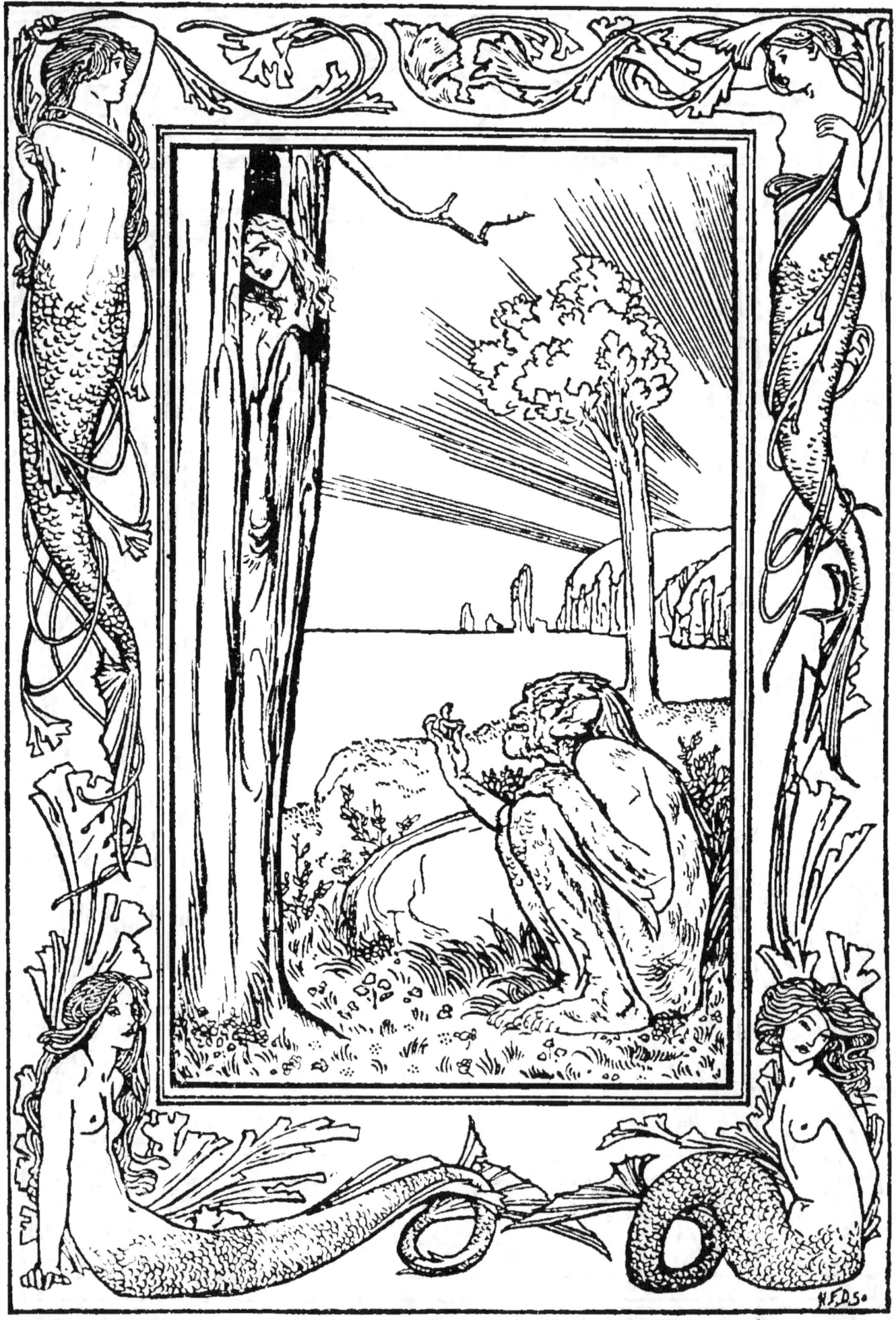

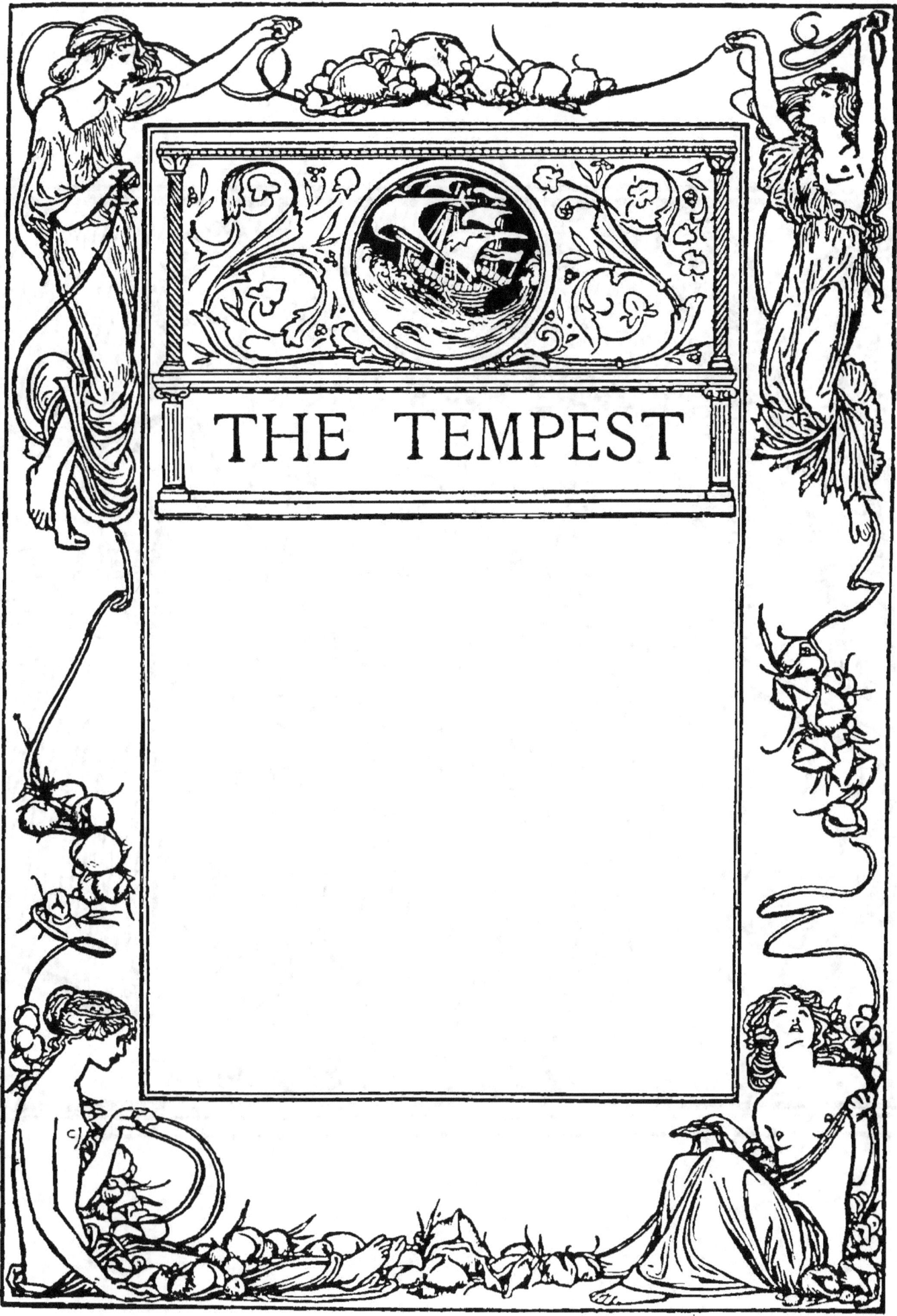

THE TEMPEST

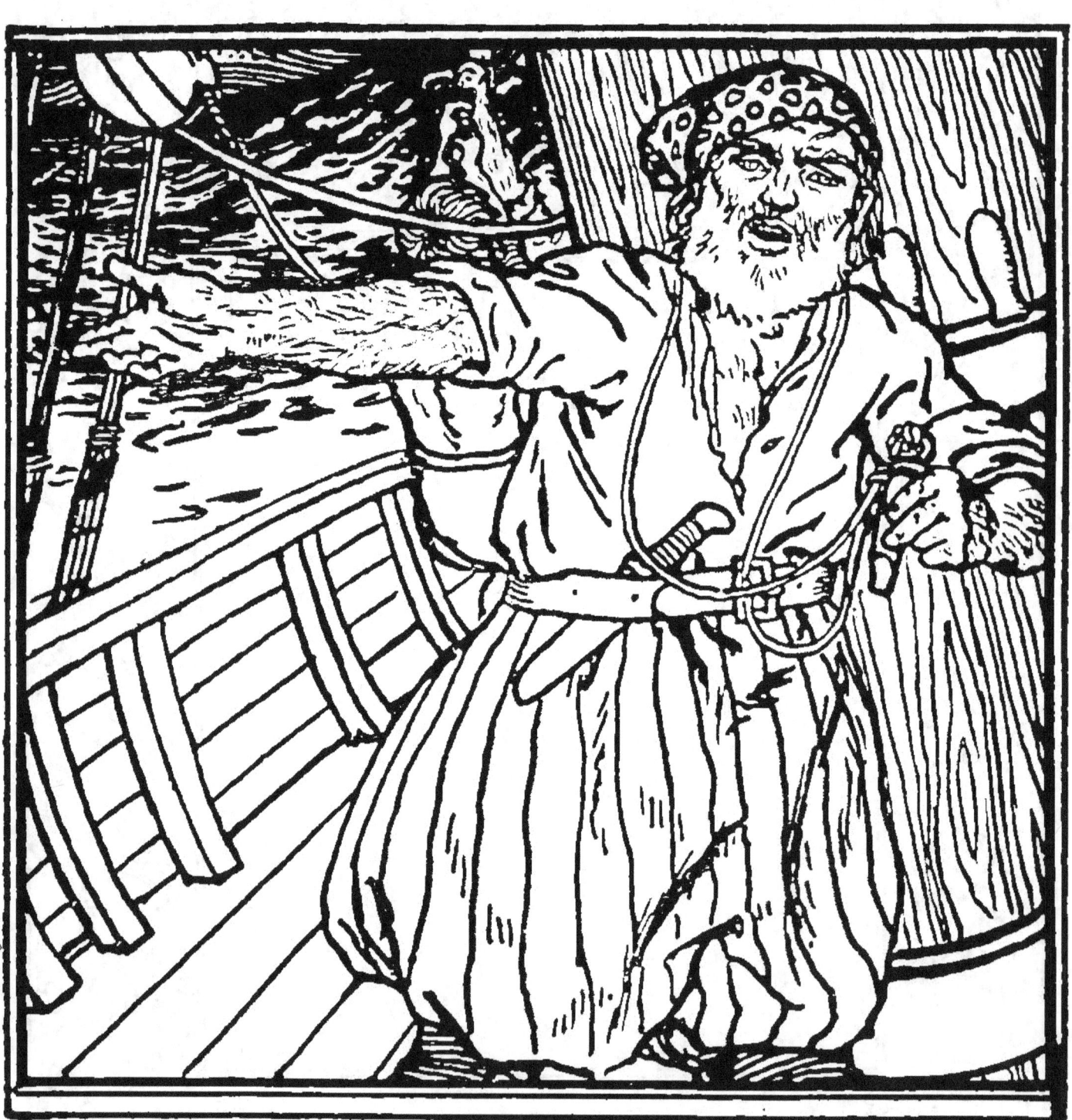

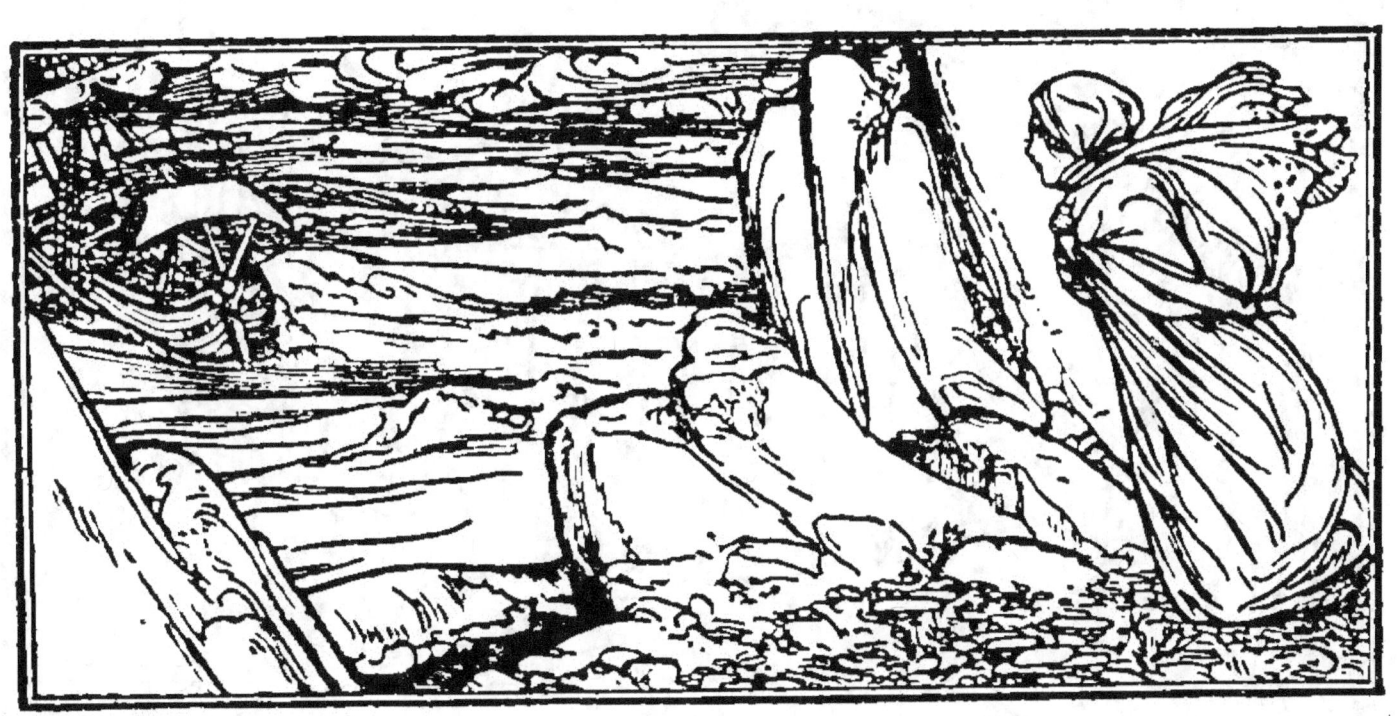

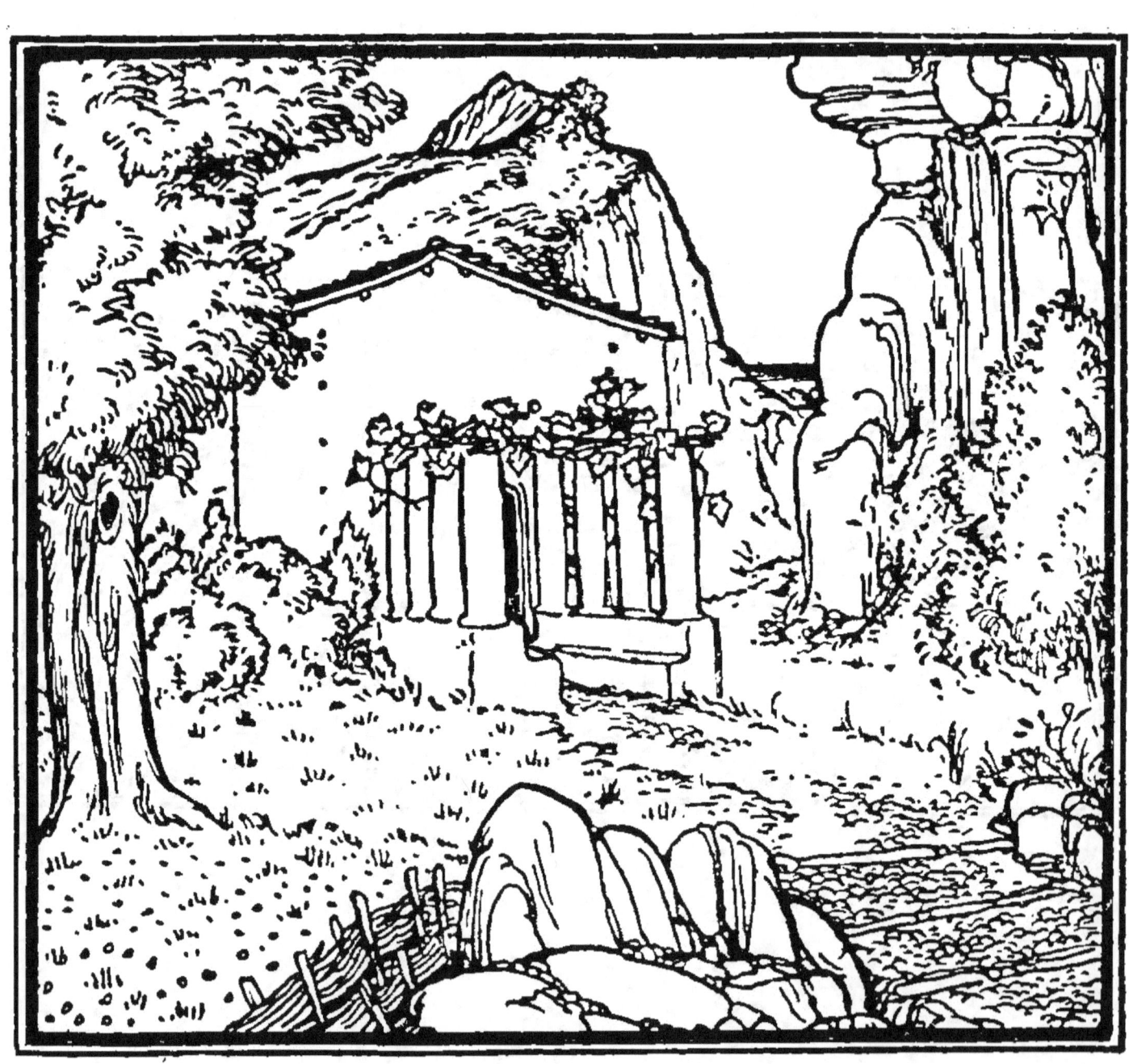

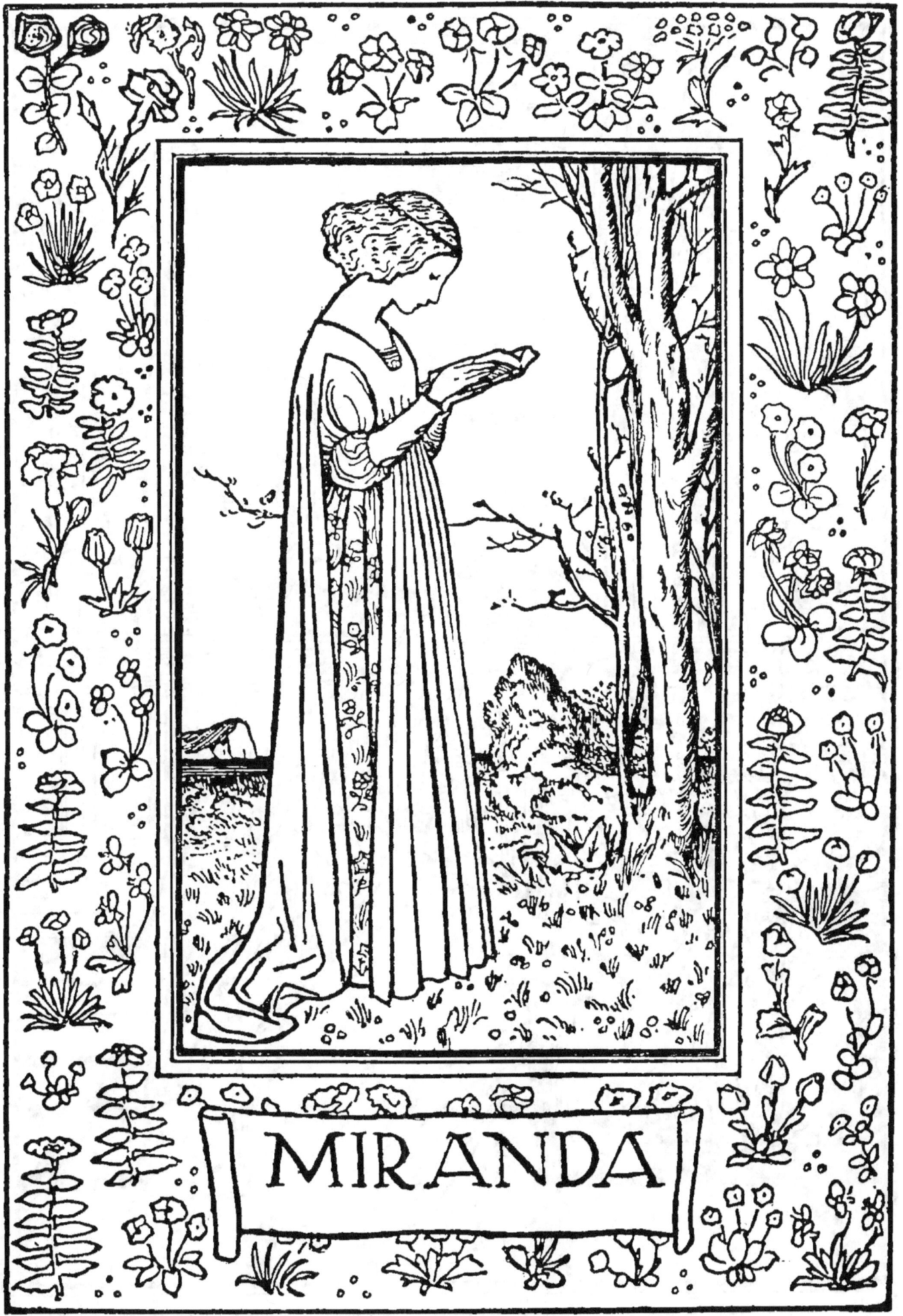

MIRANDA

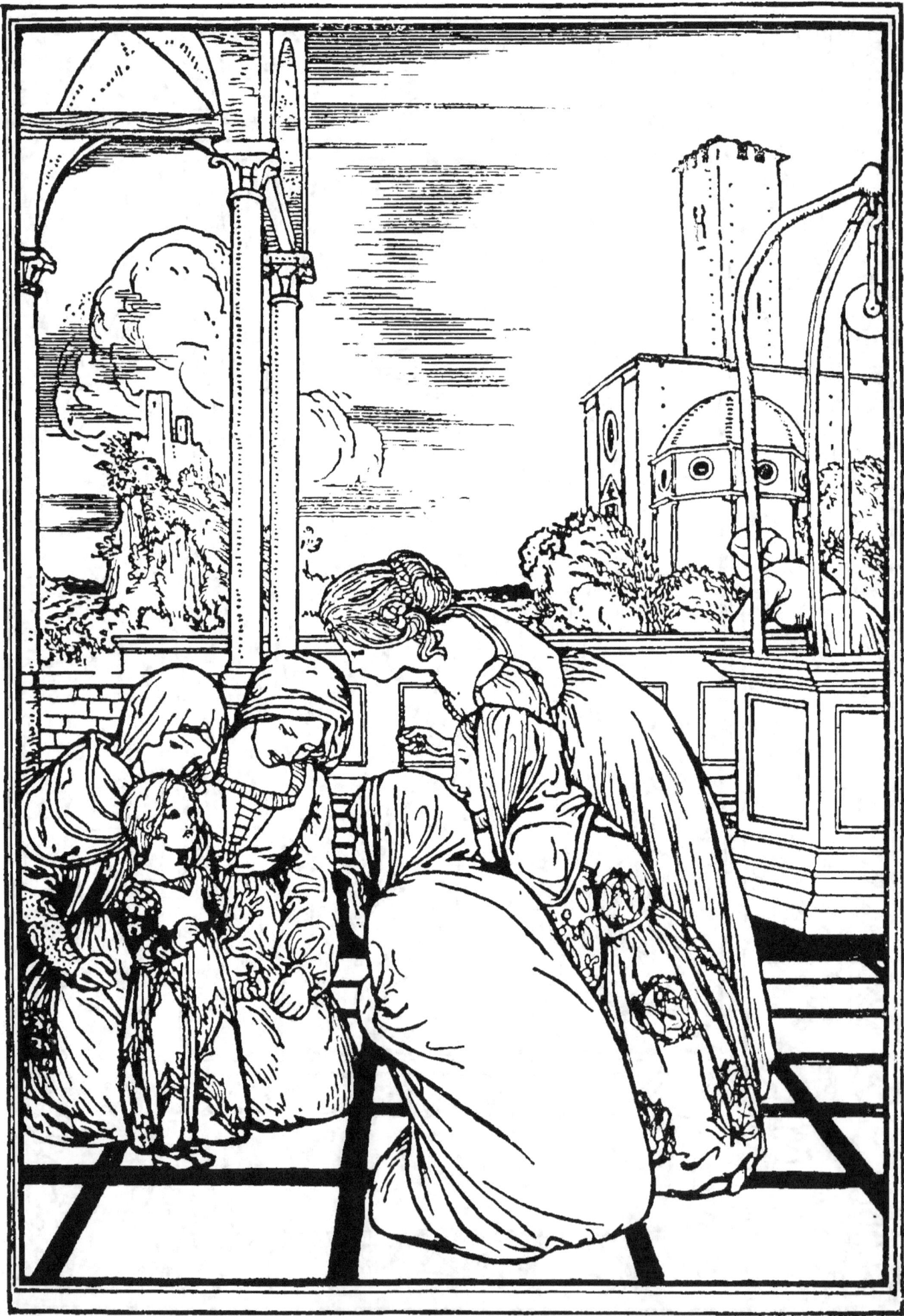

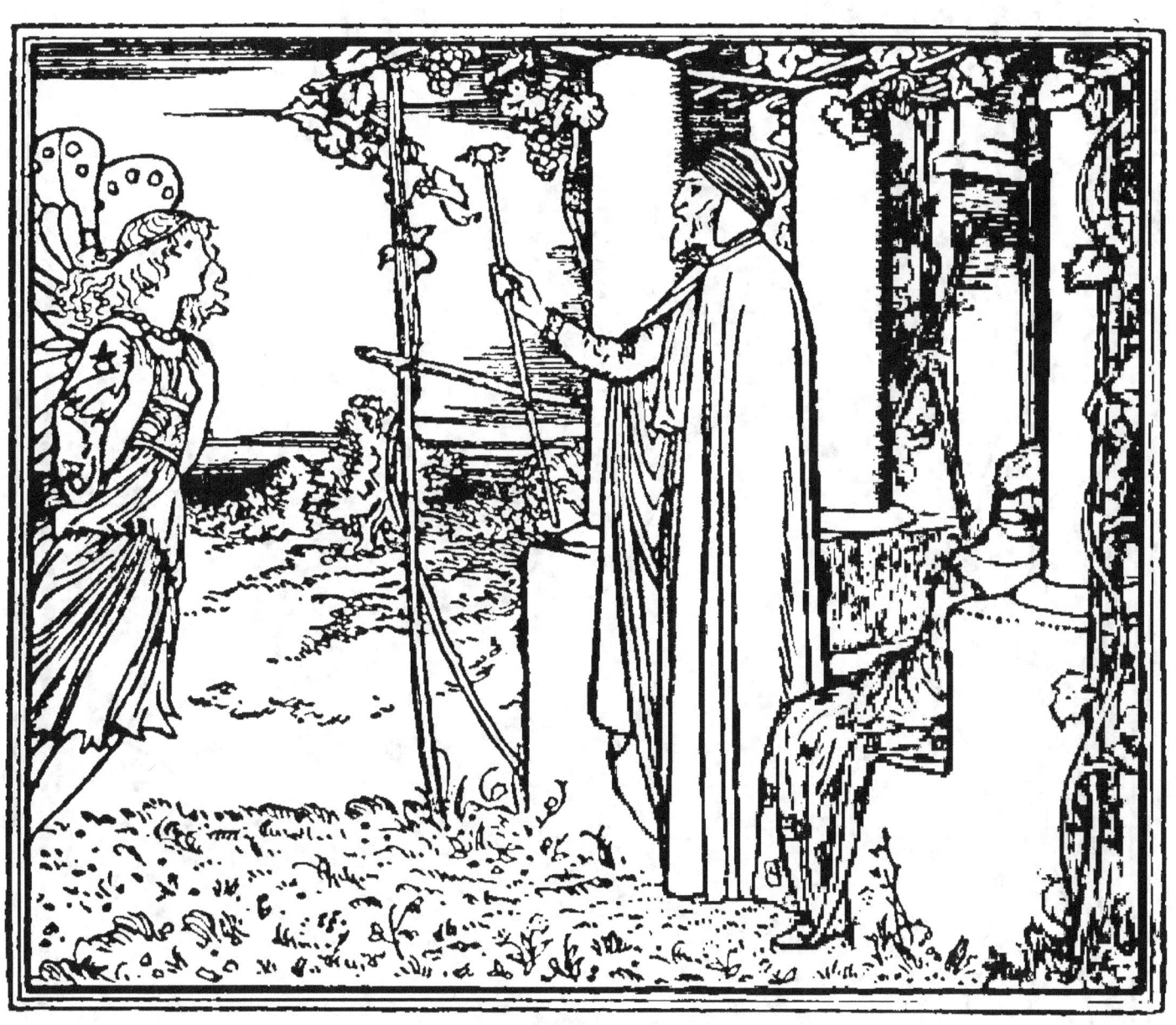

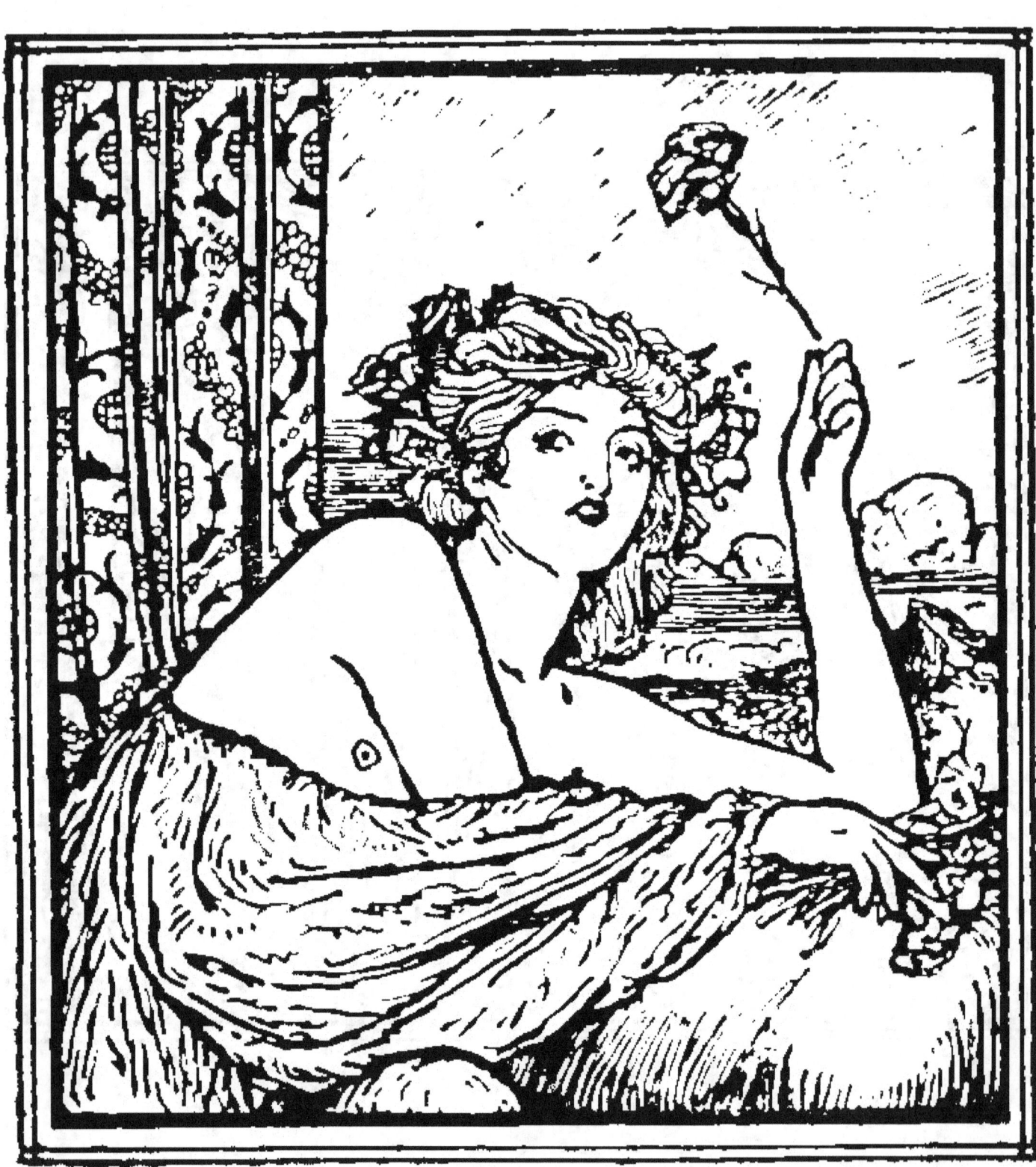

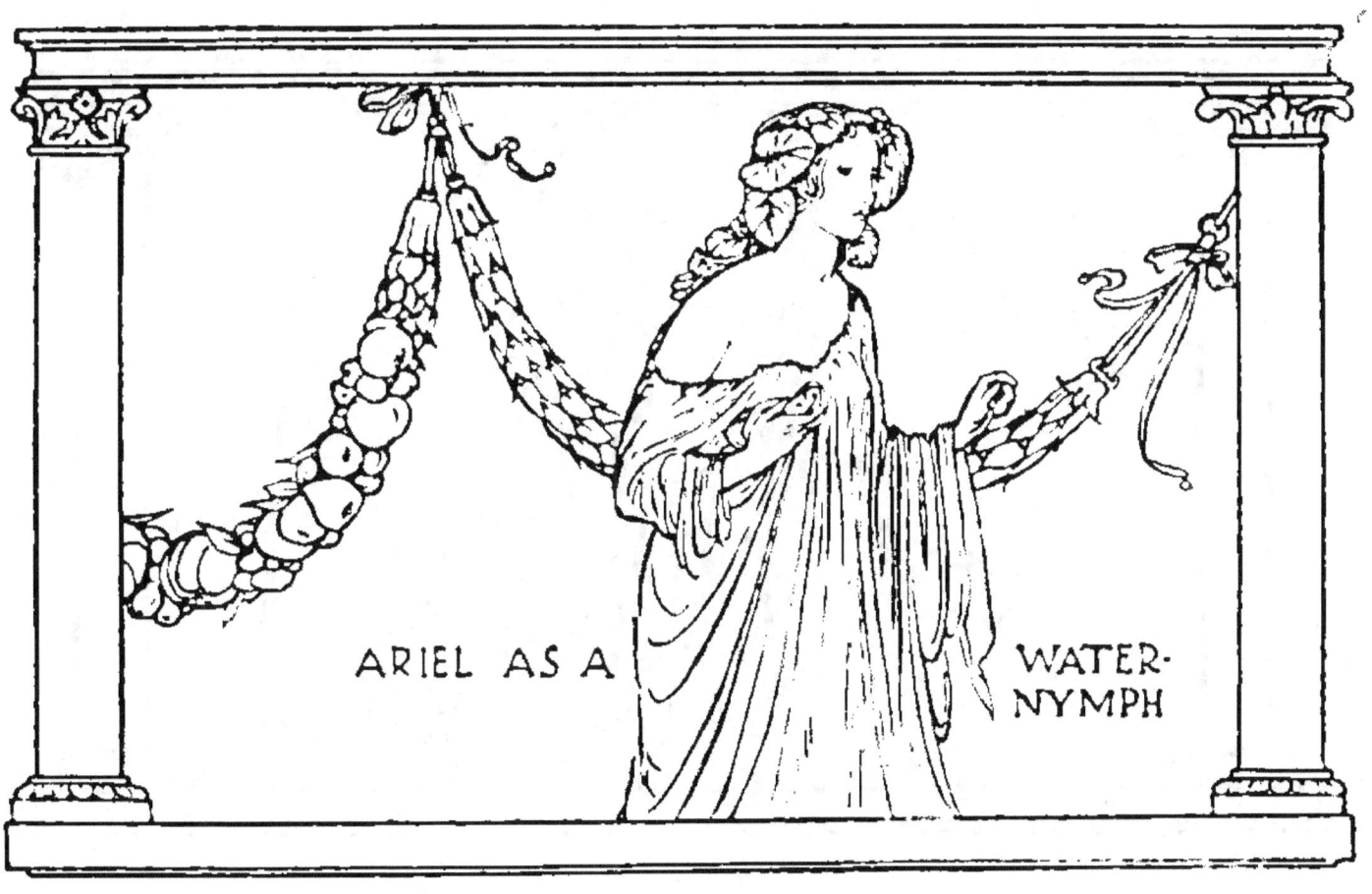

ARIEL AS A WATER-NYMPH

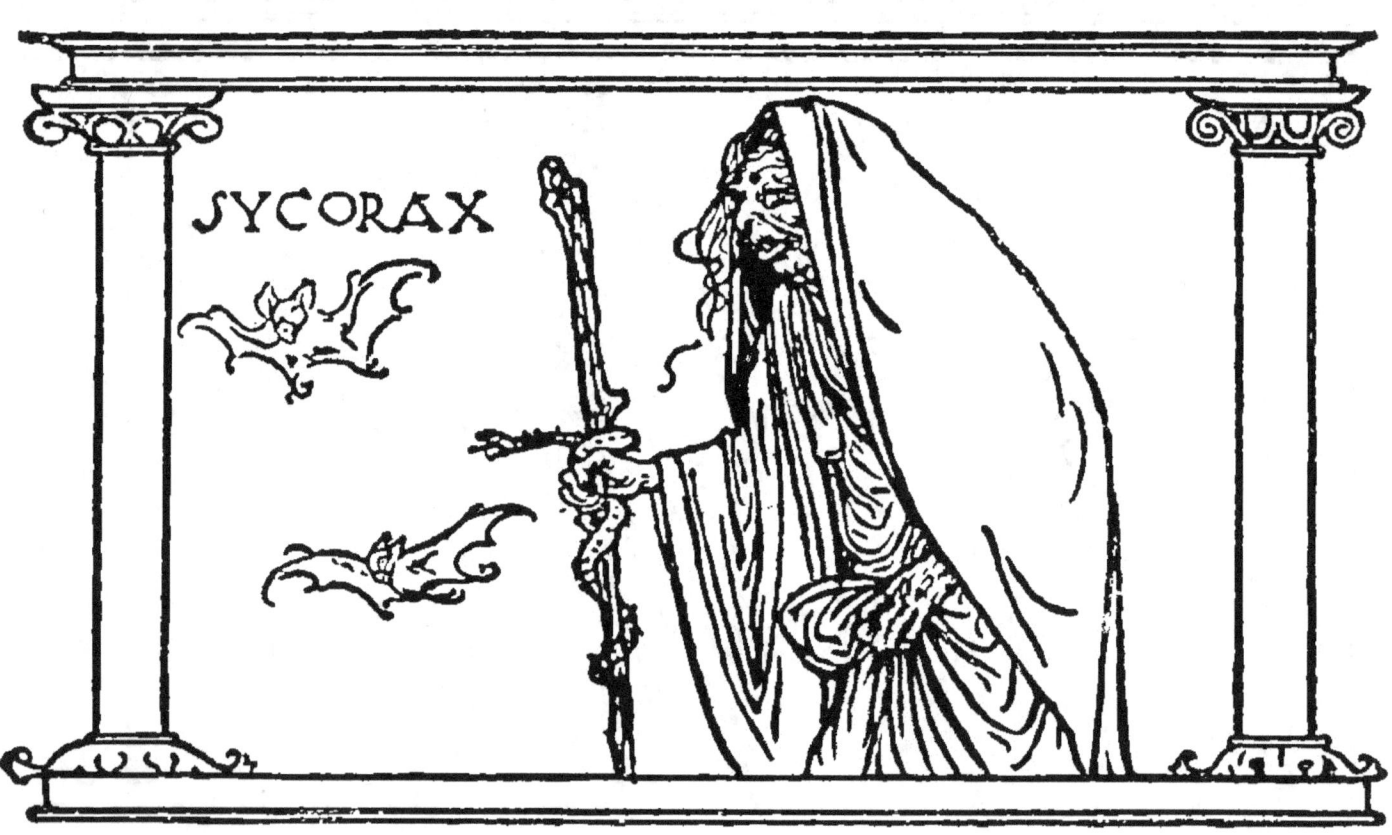

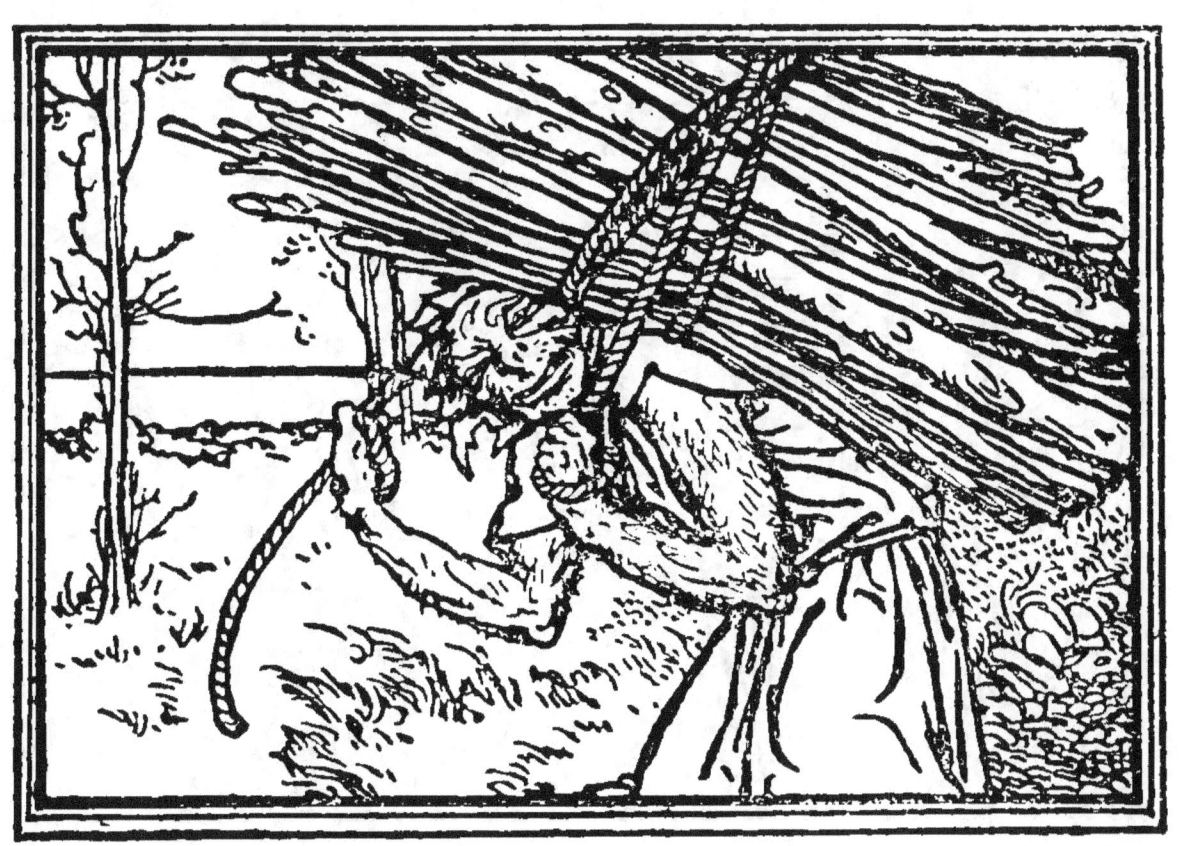

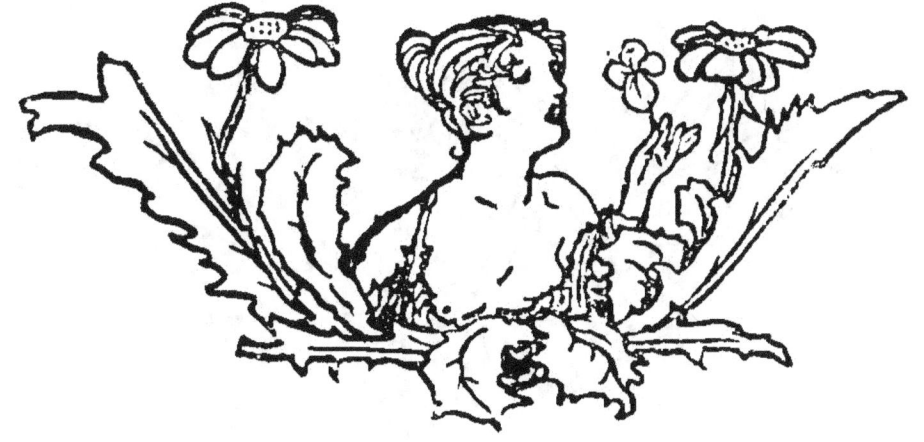

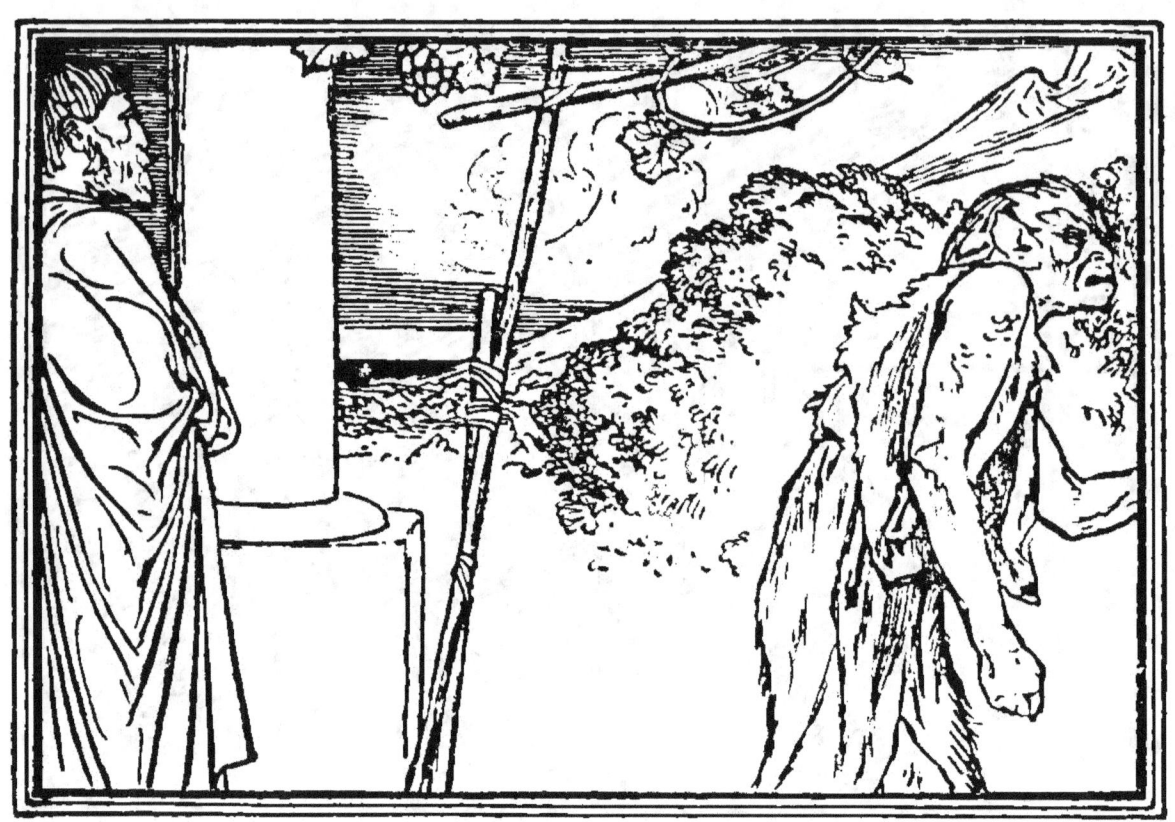

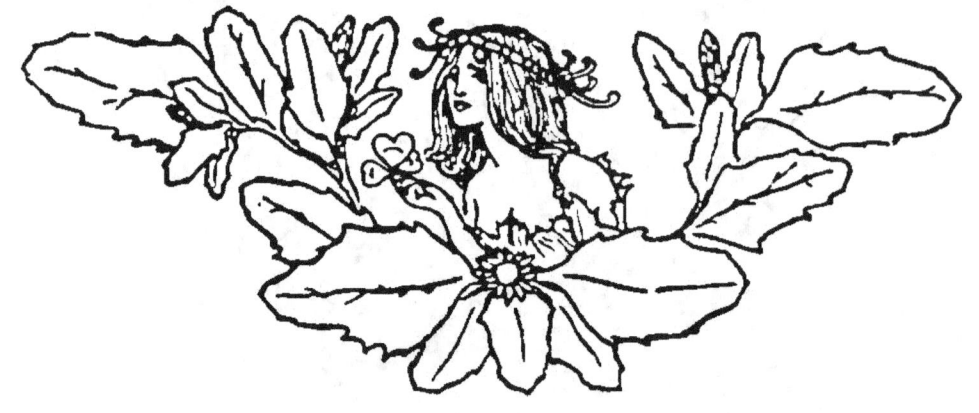

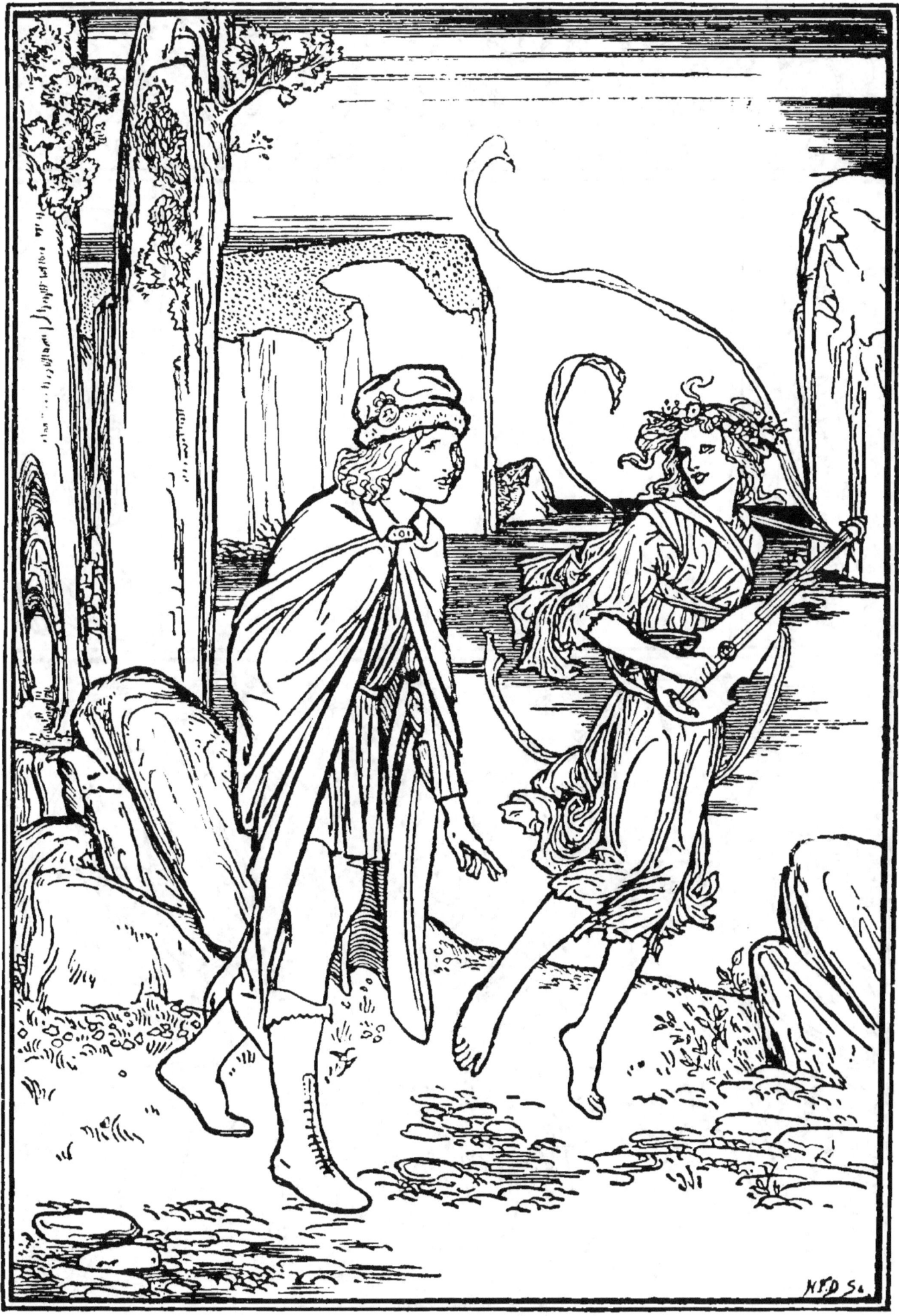

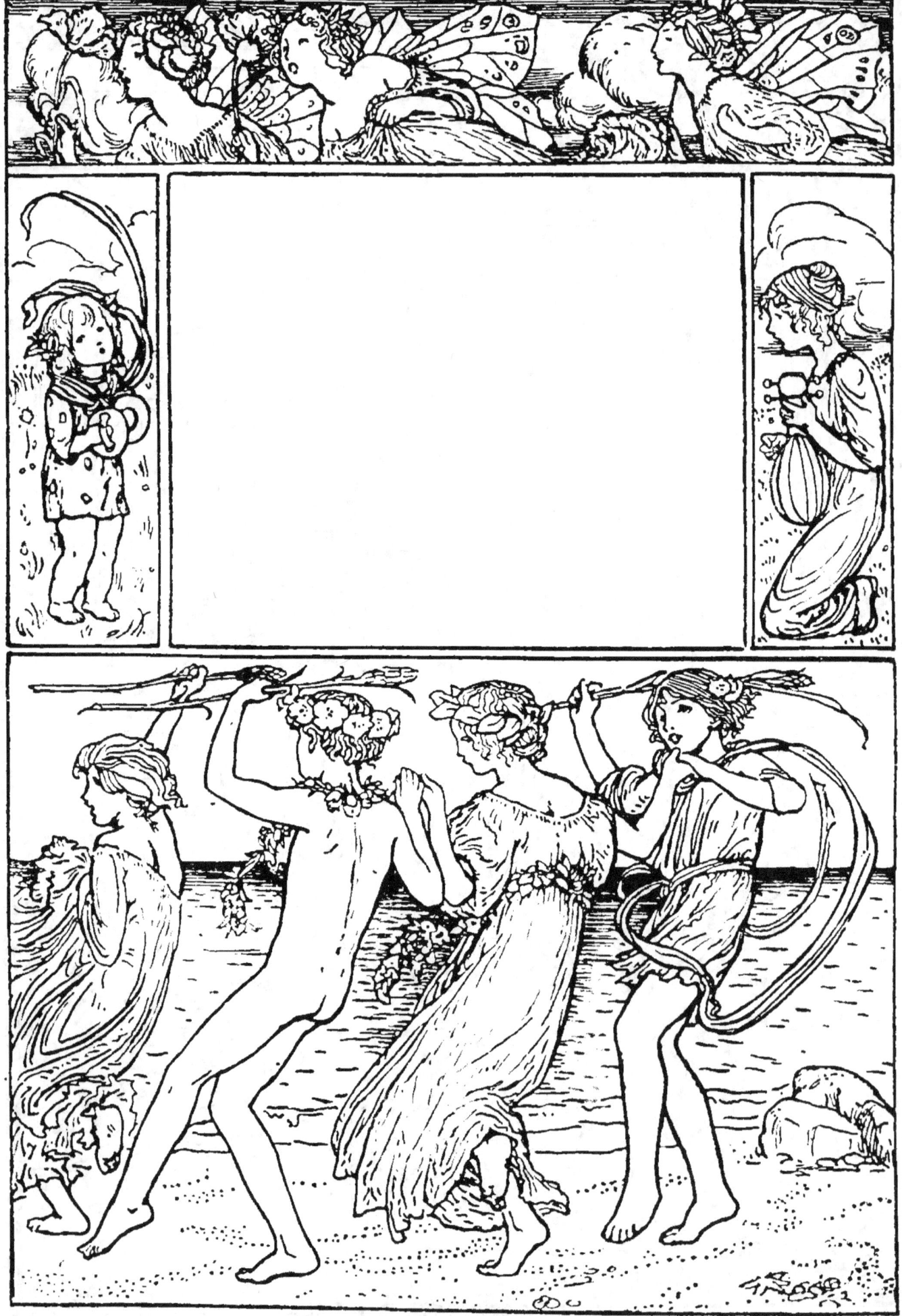

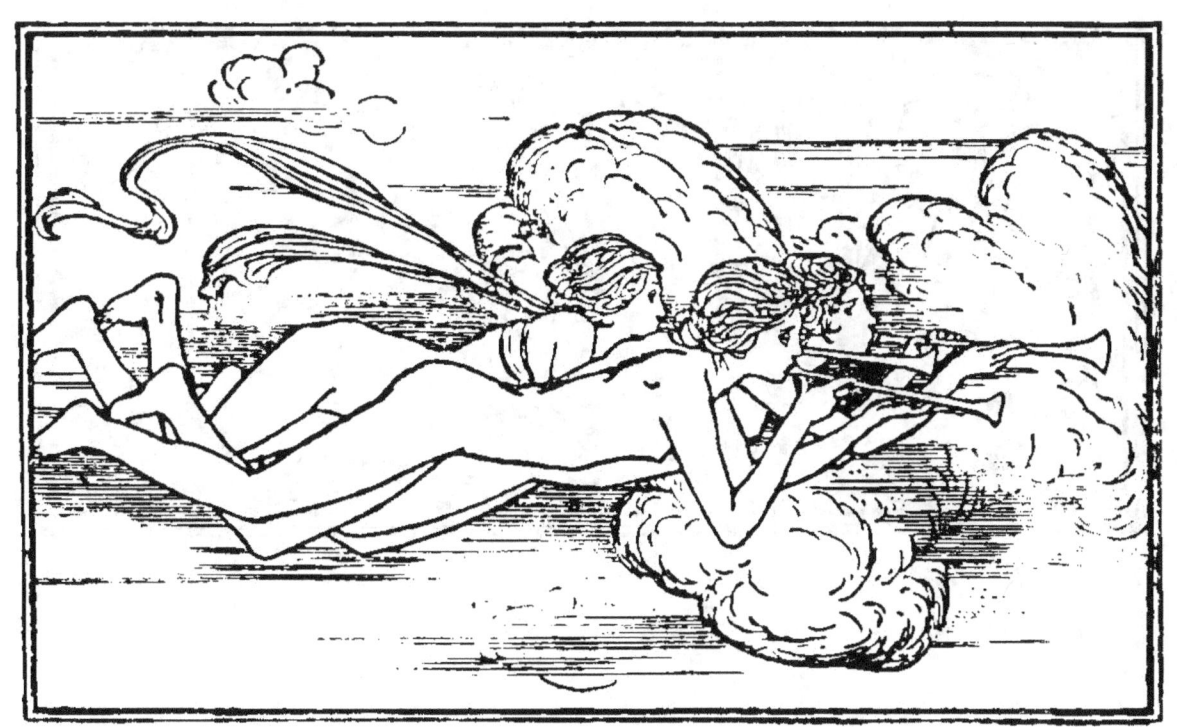

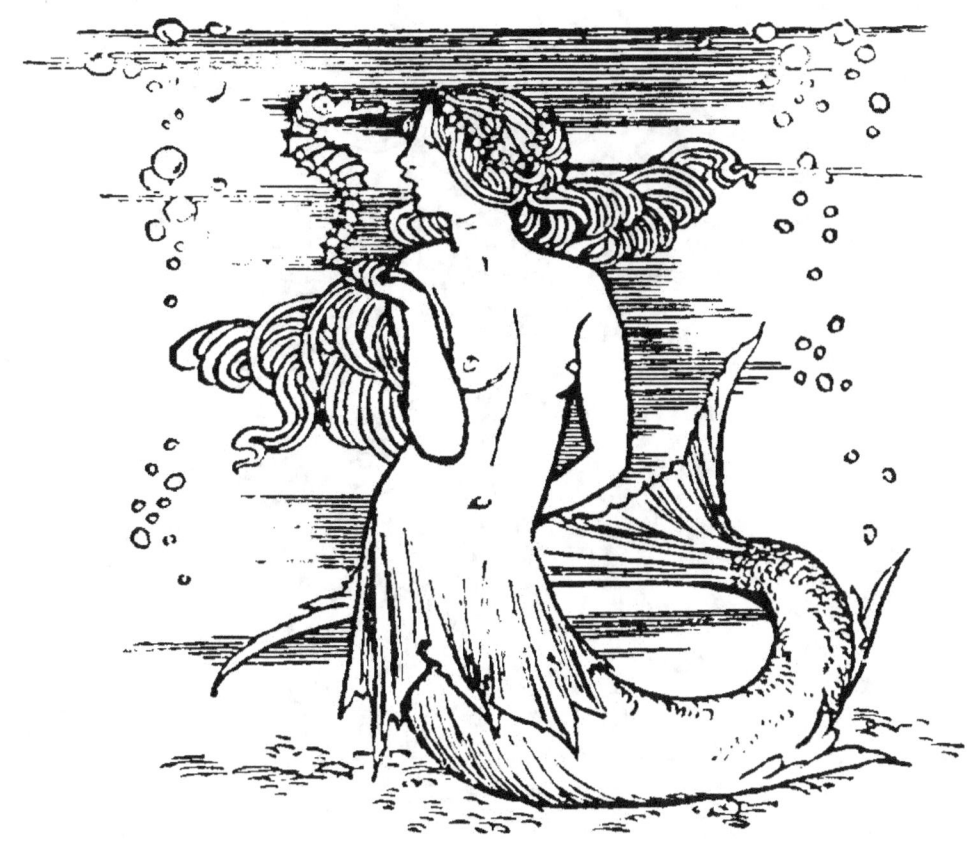

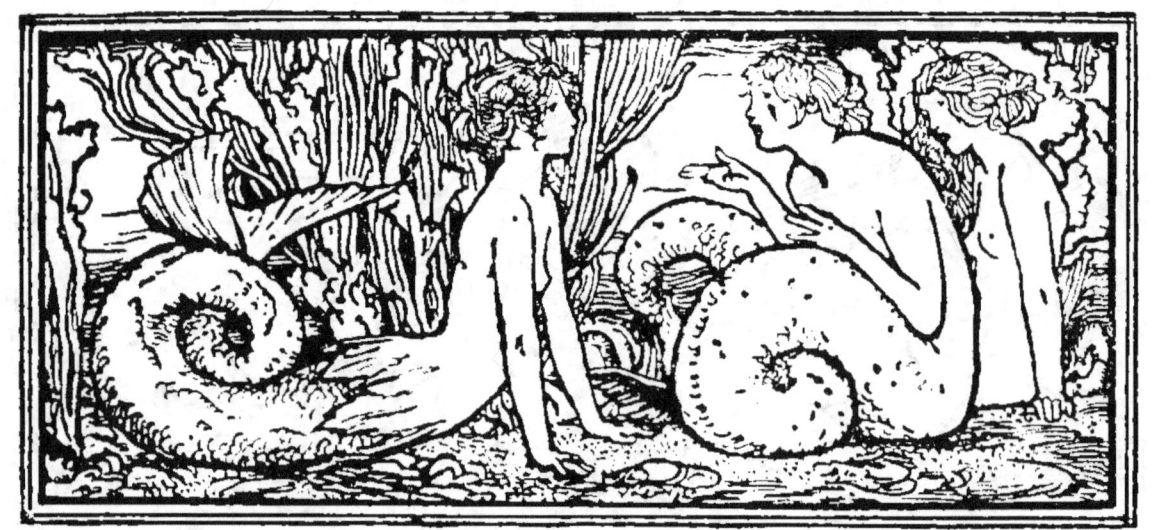

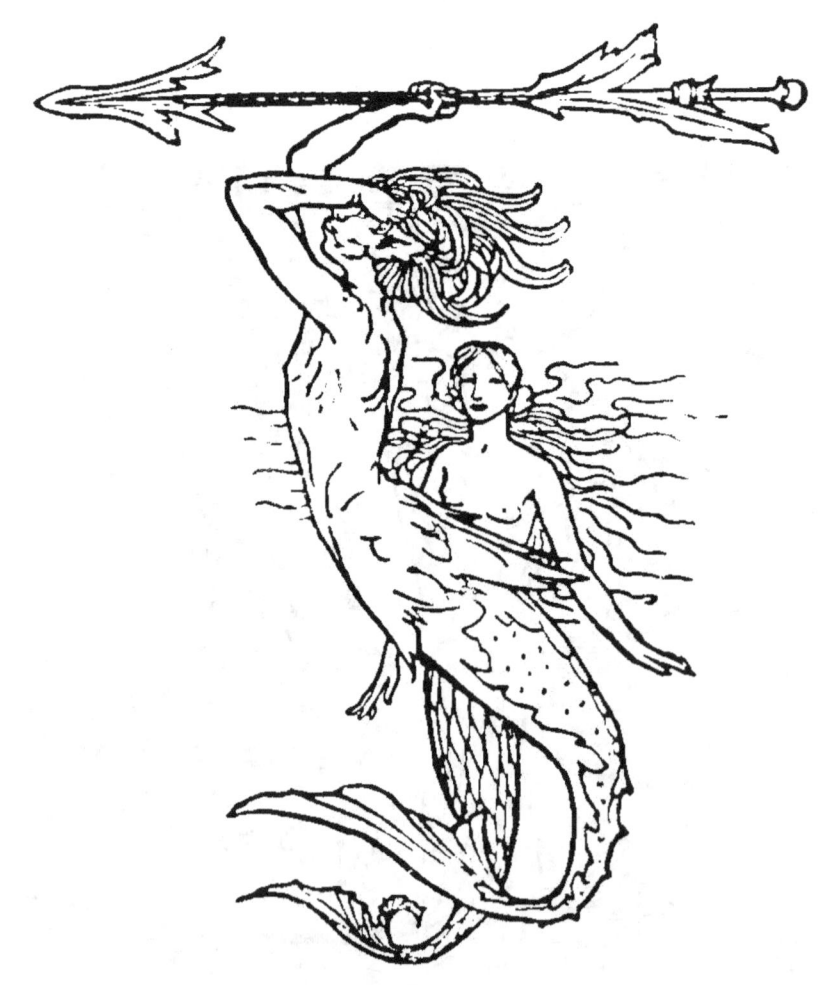

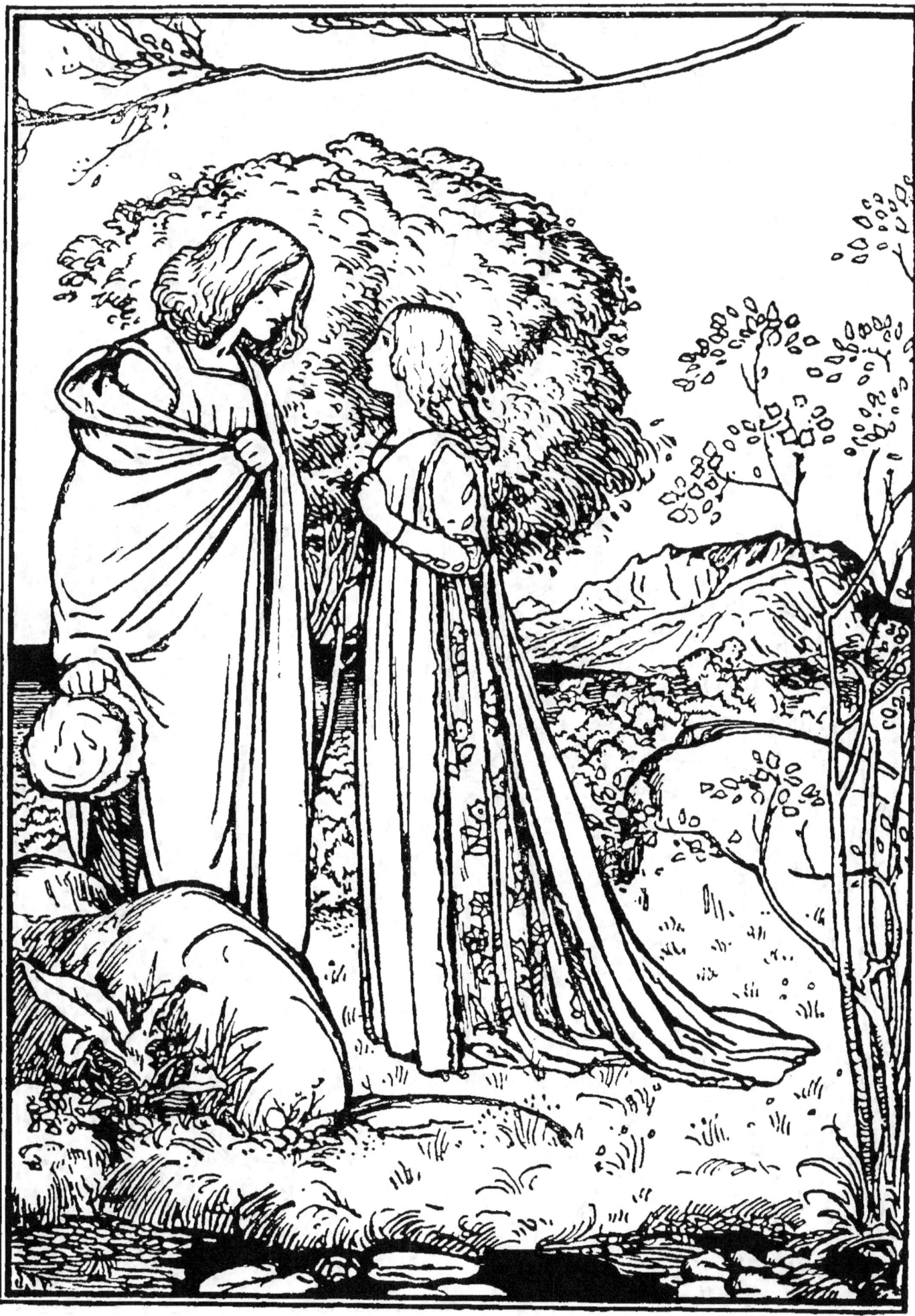

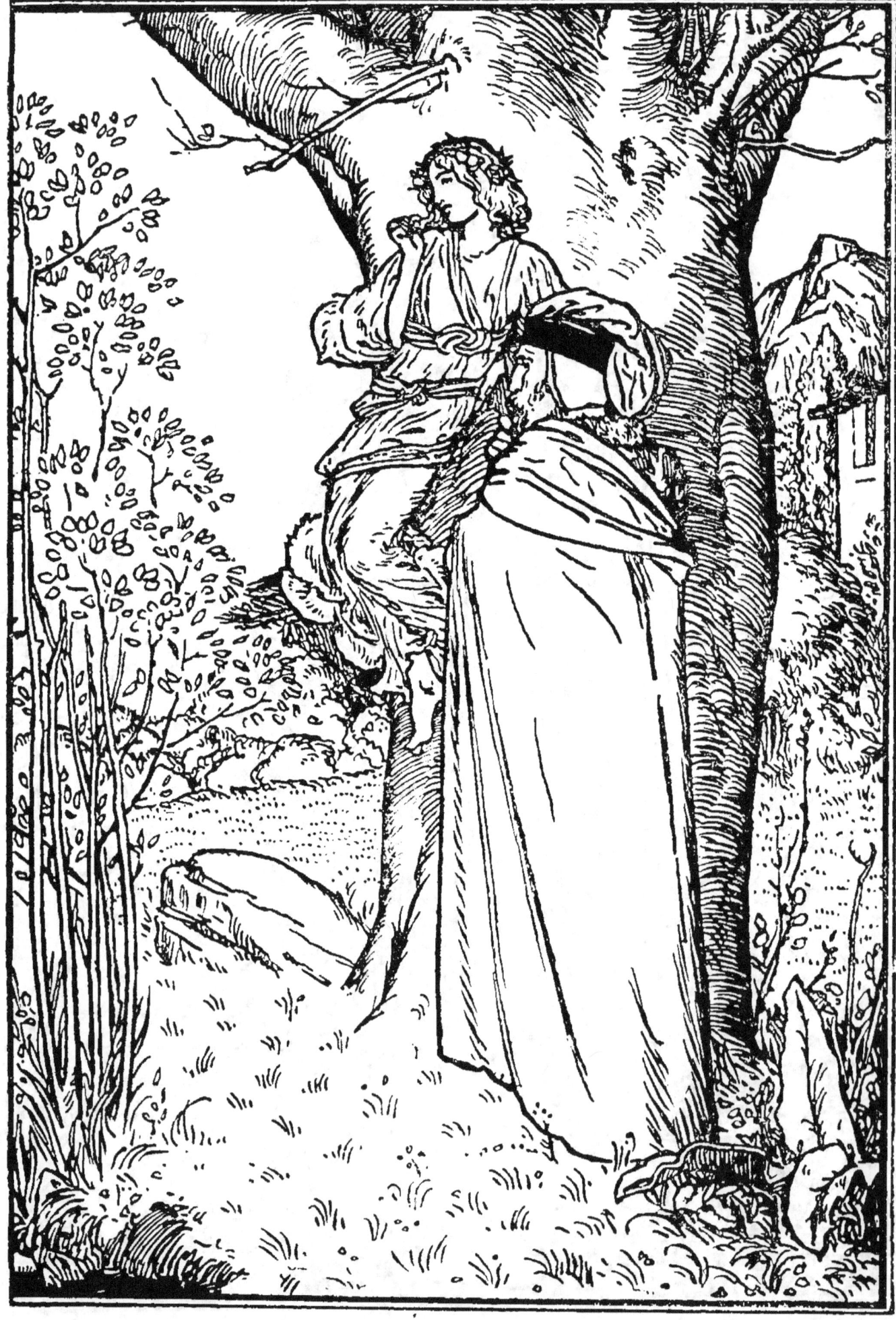

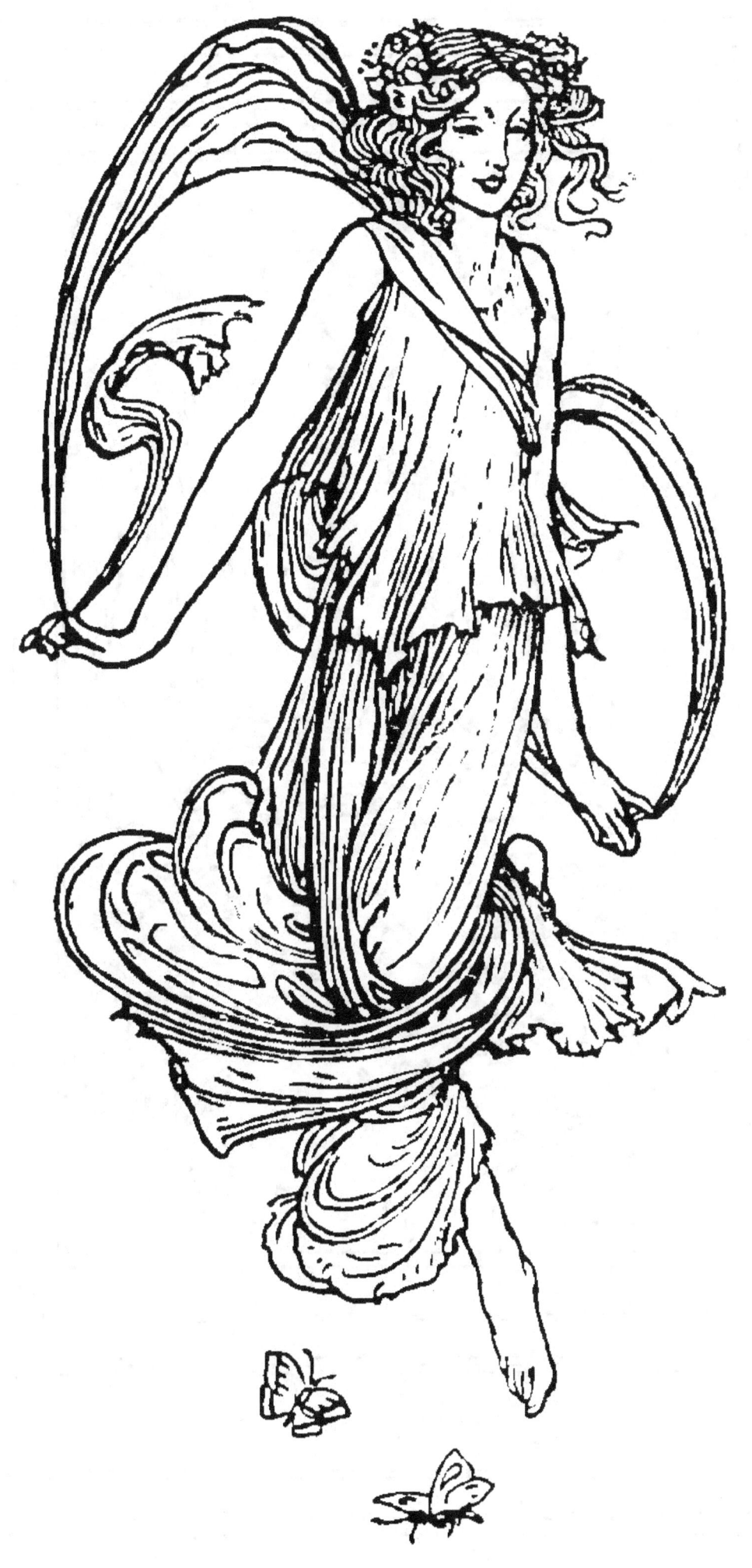

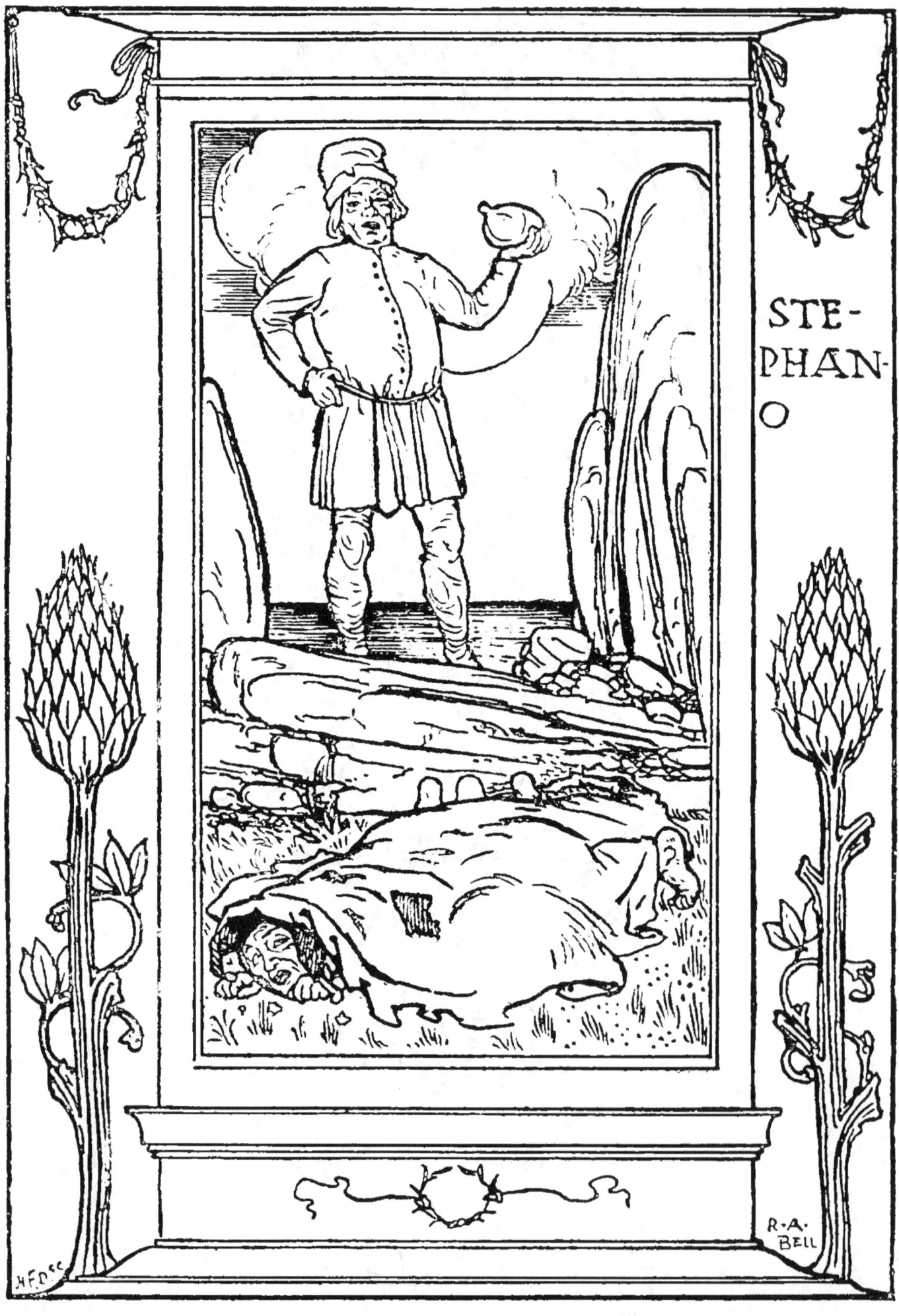

STE-
PHAN-
O

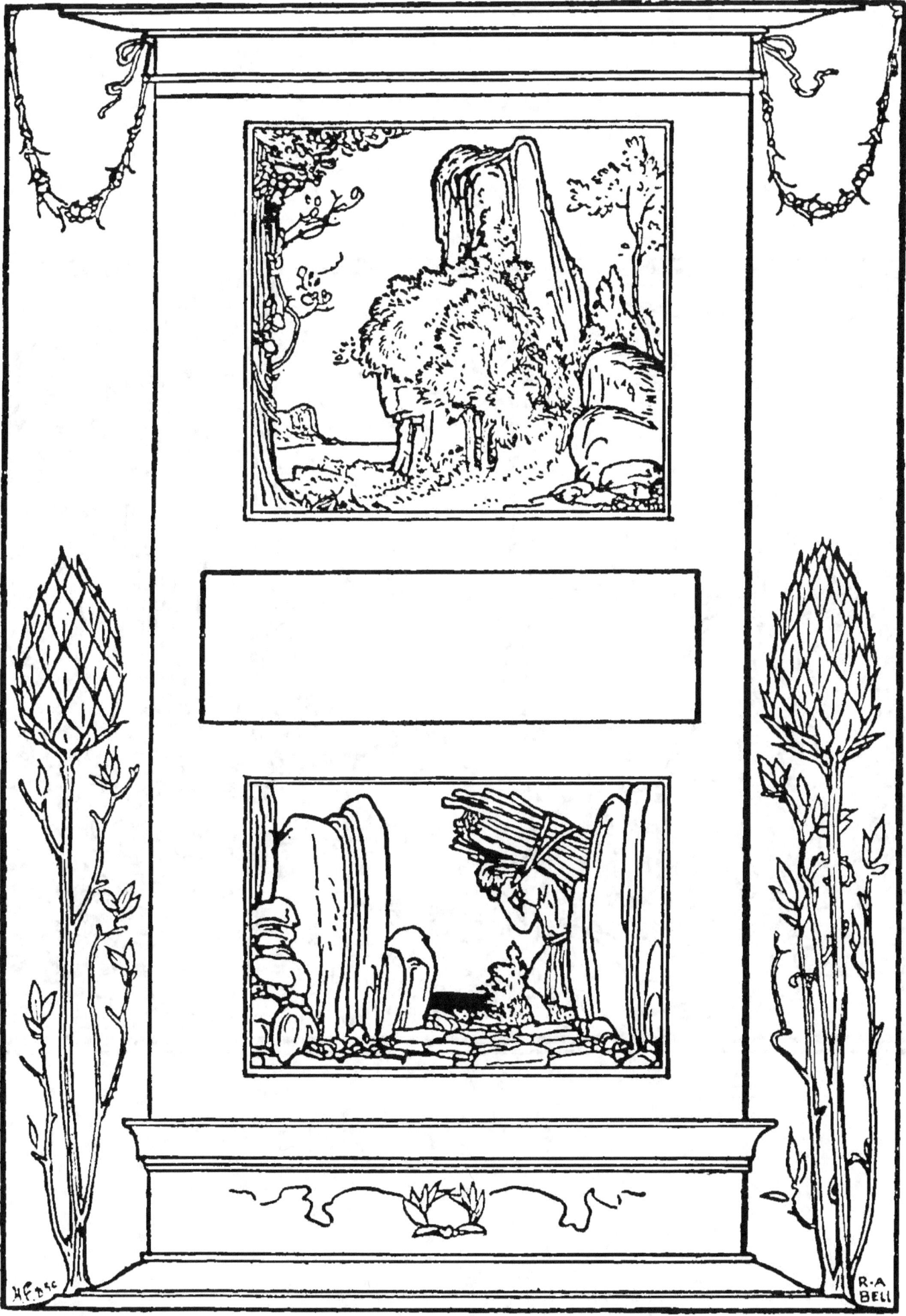

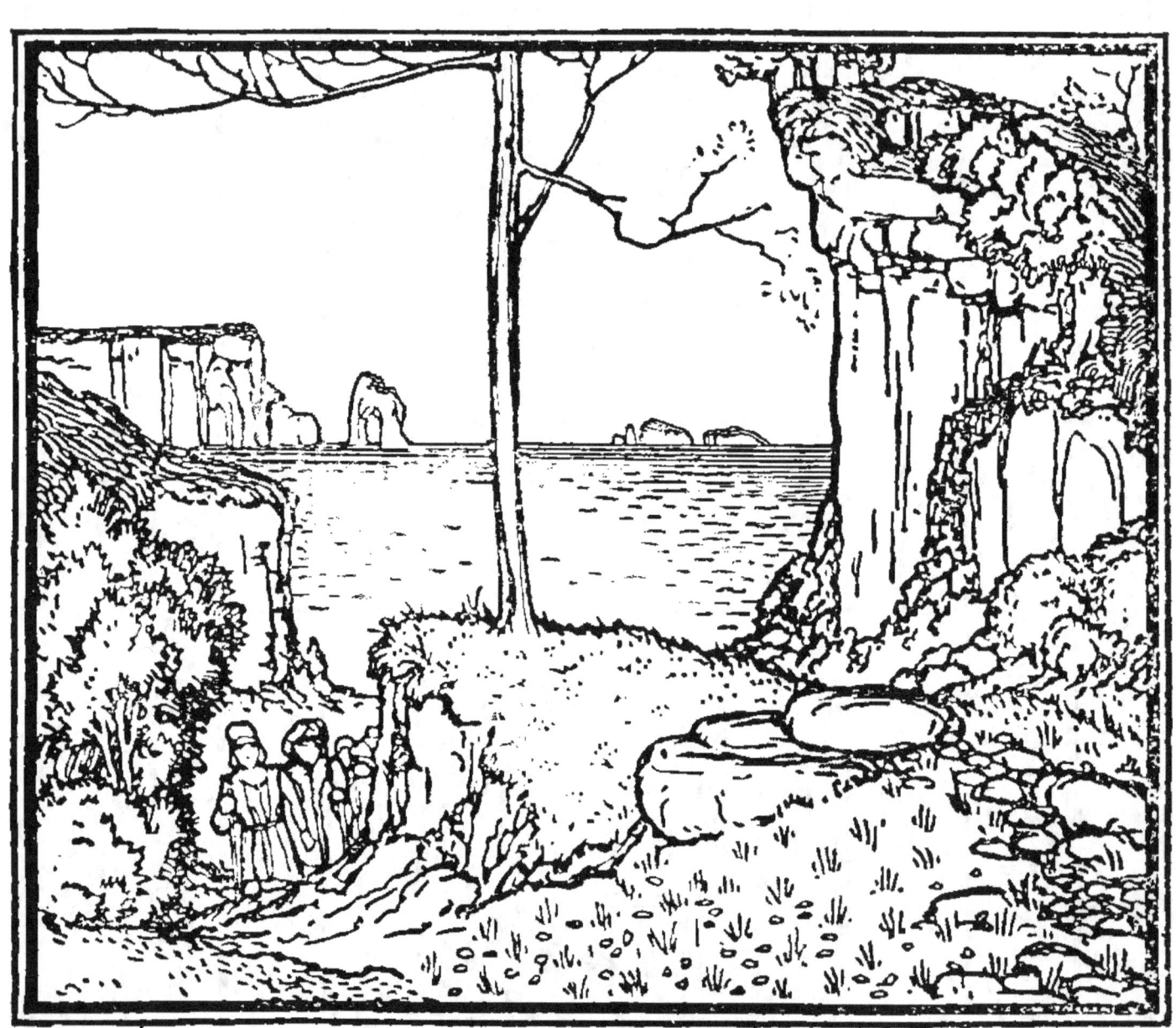

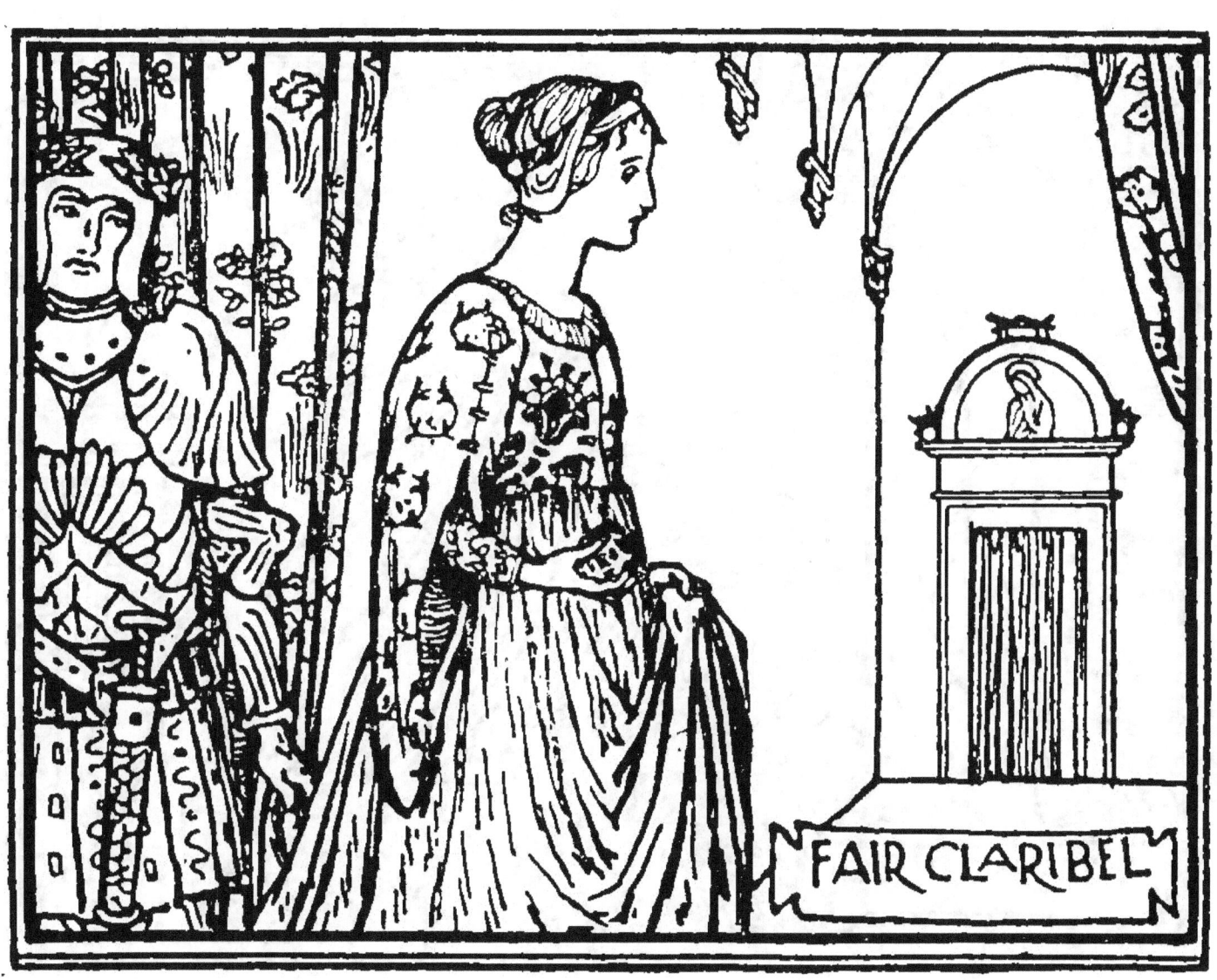

FAIR CLARIBEL

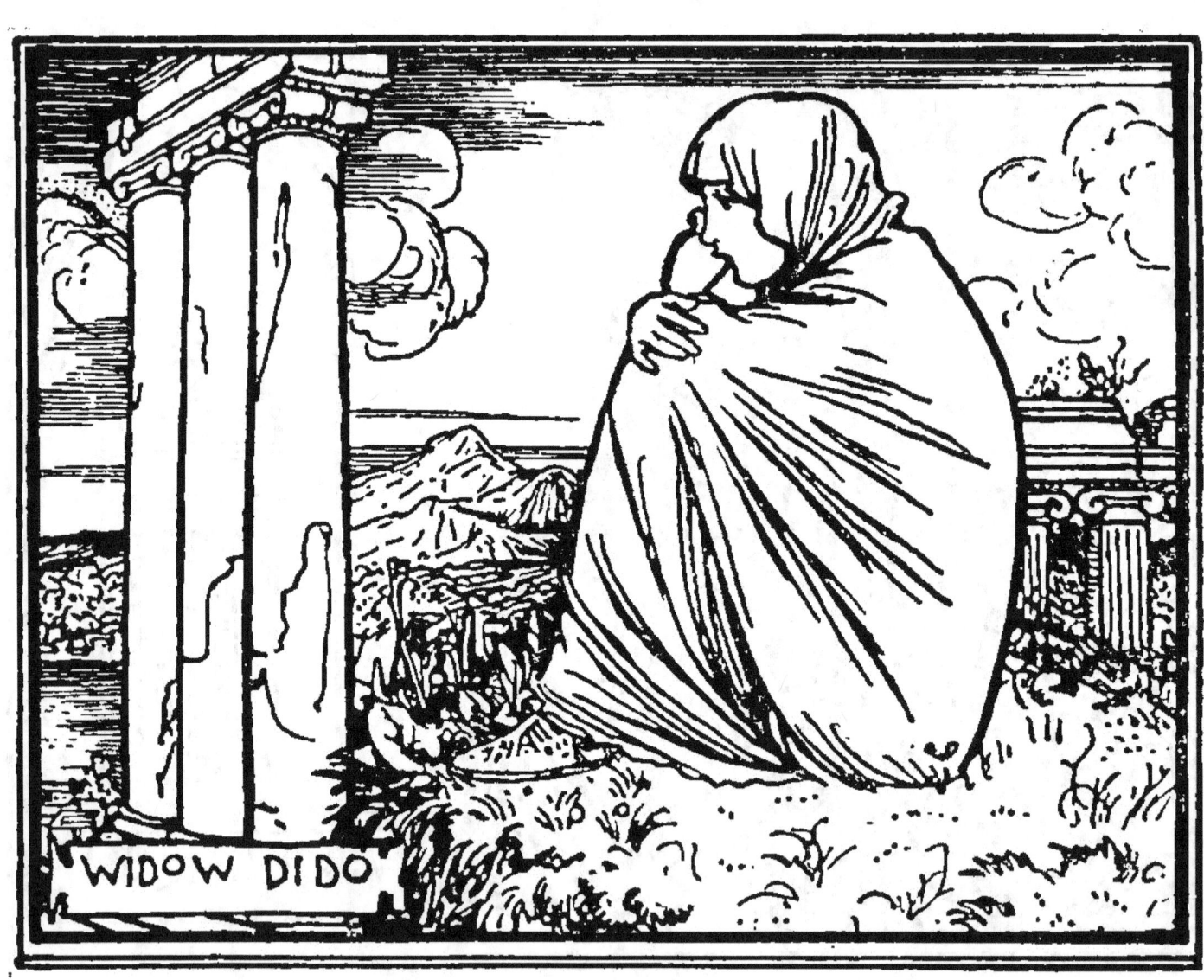

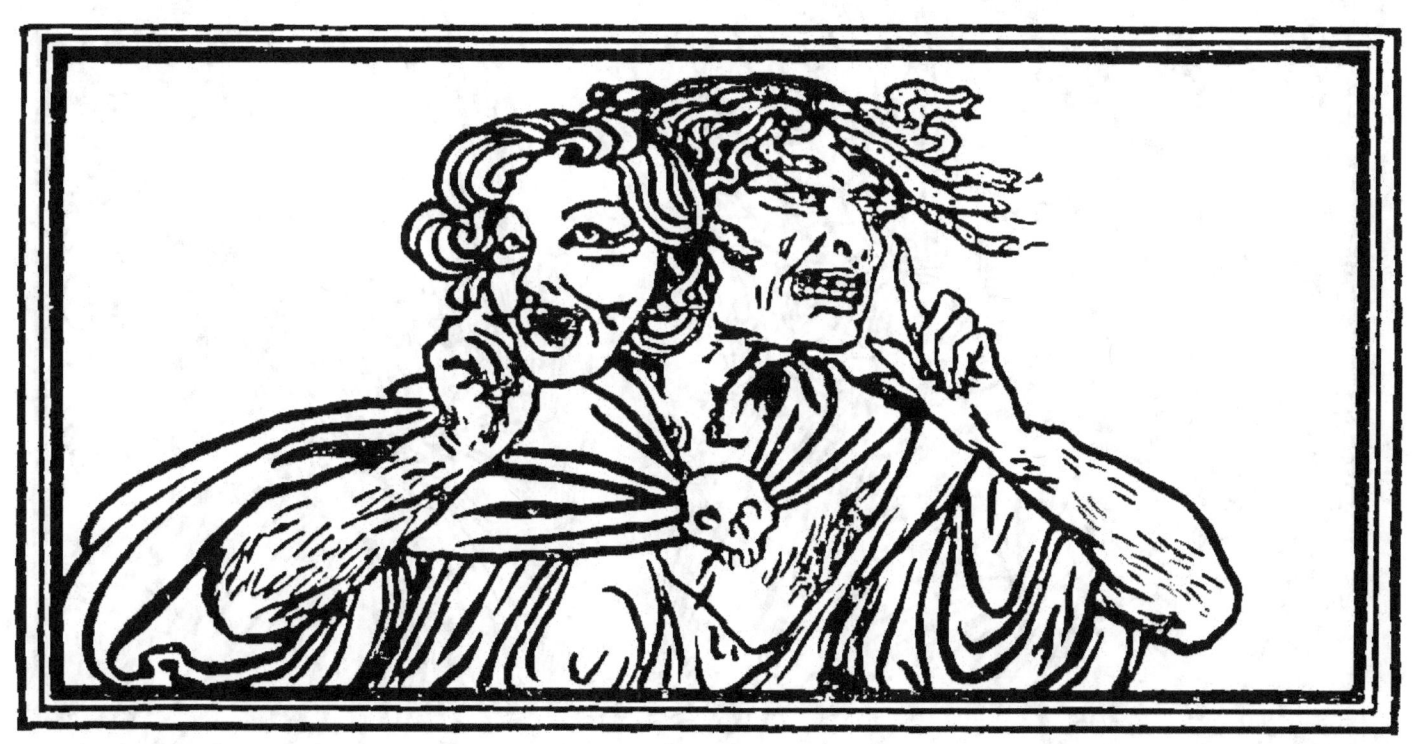

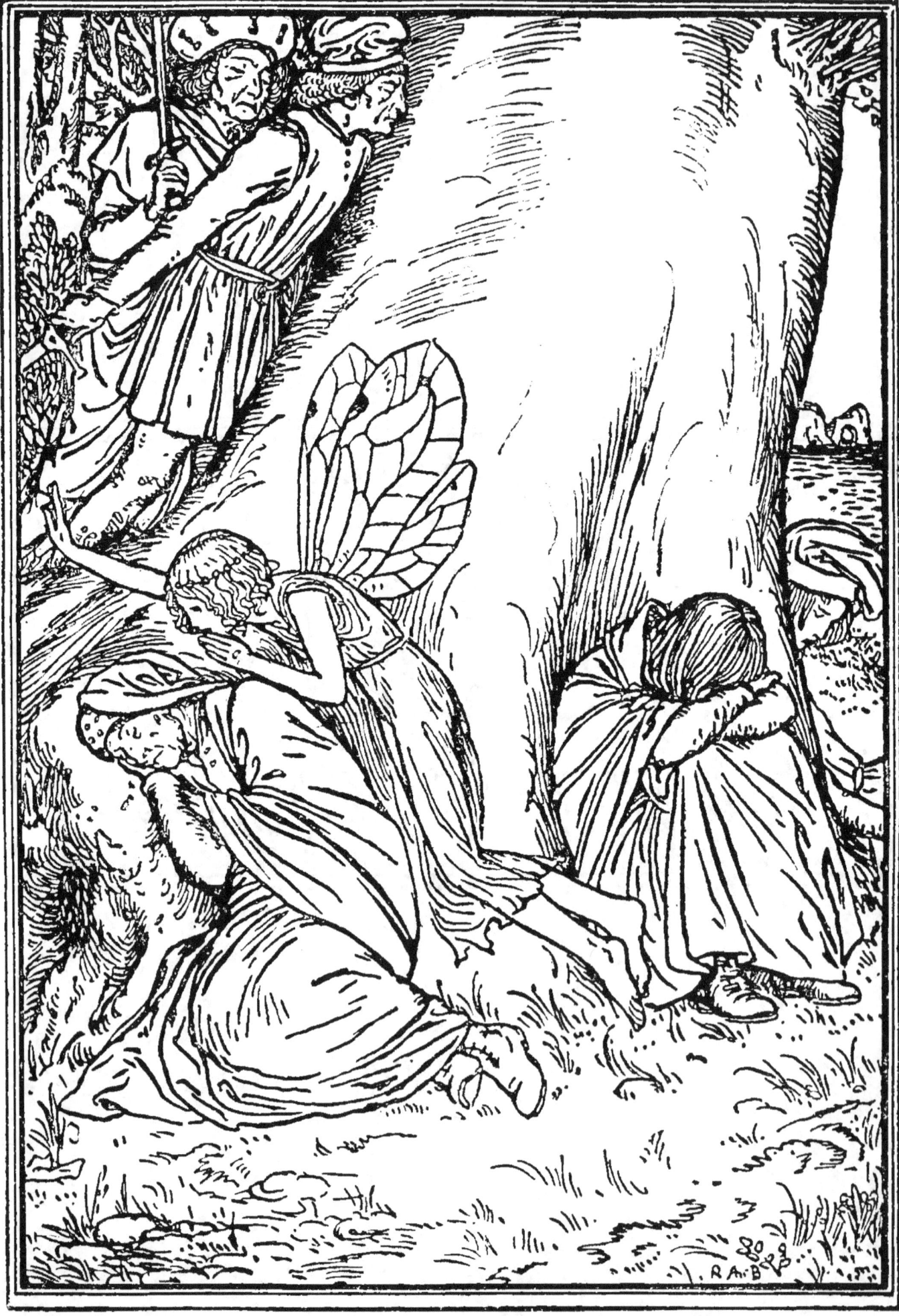

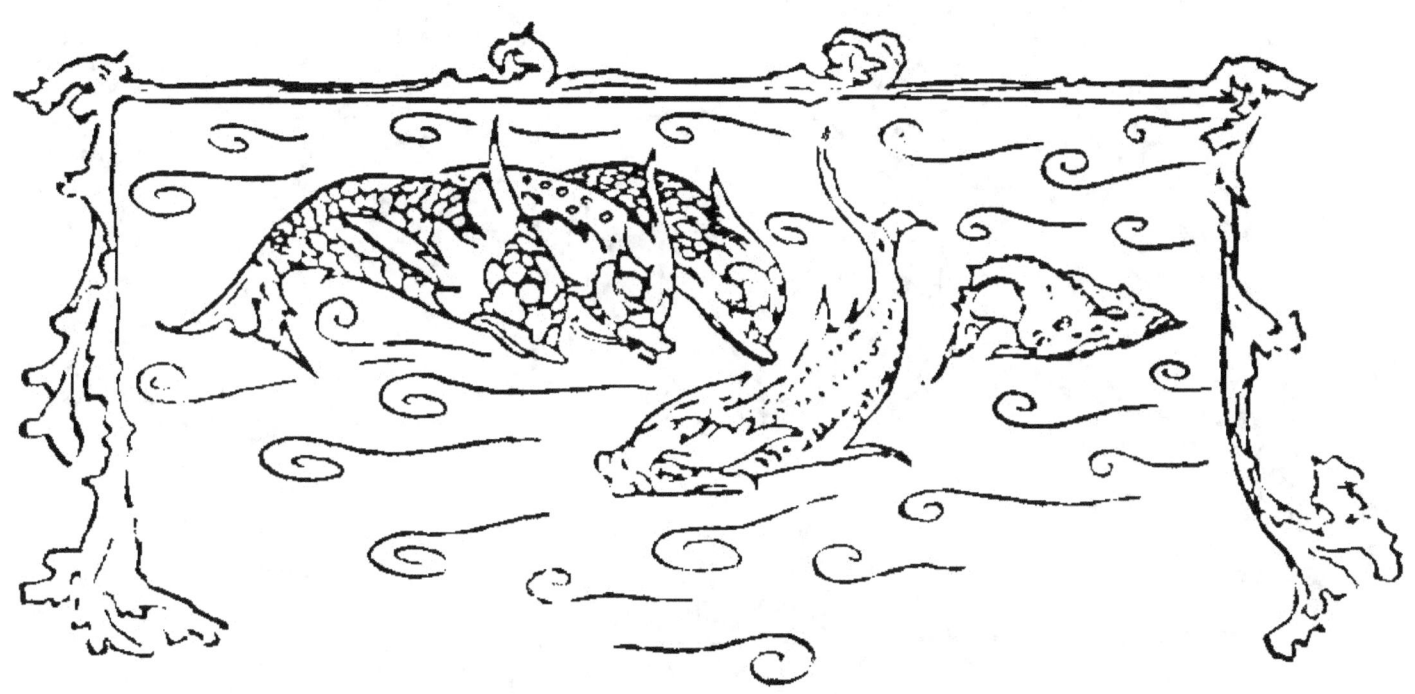

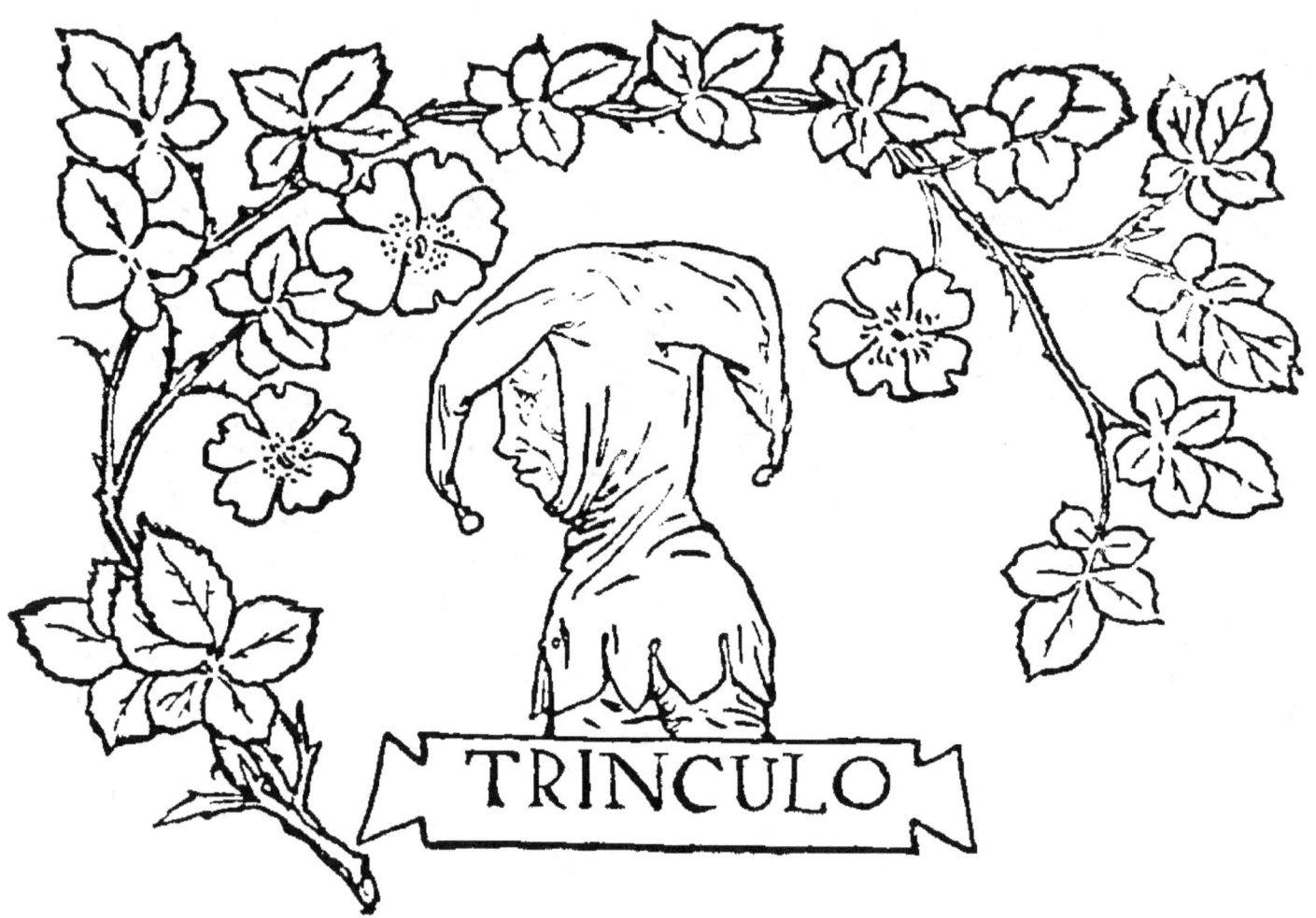

TRINCULO

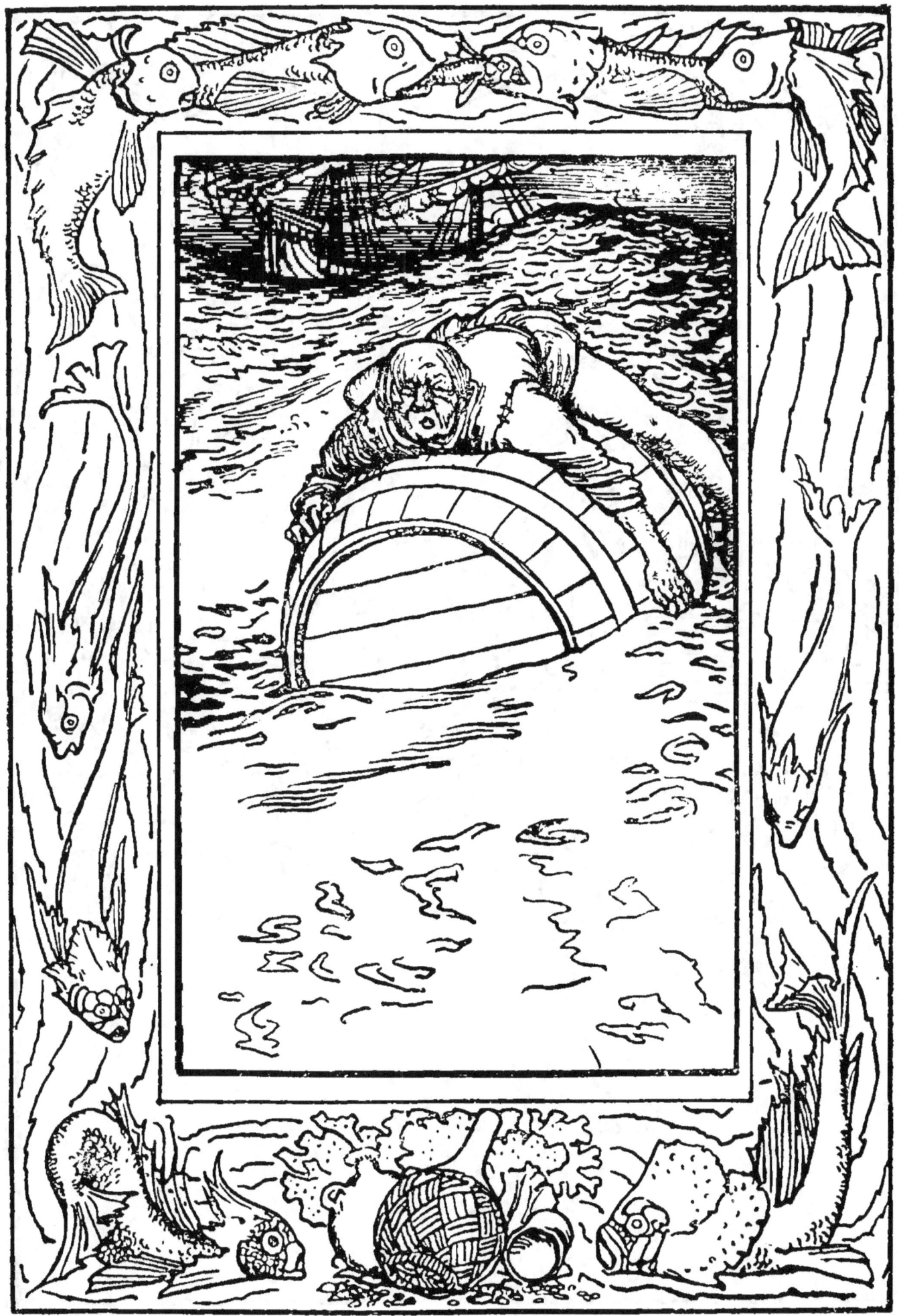

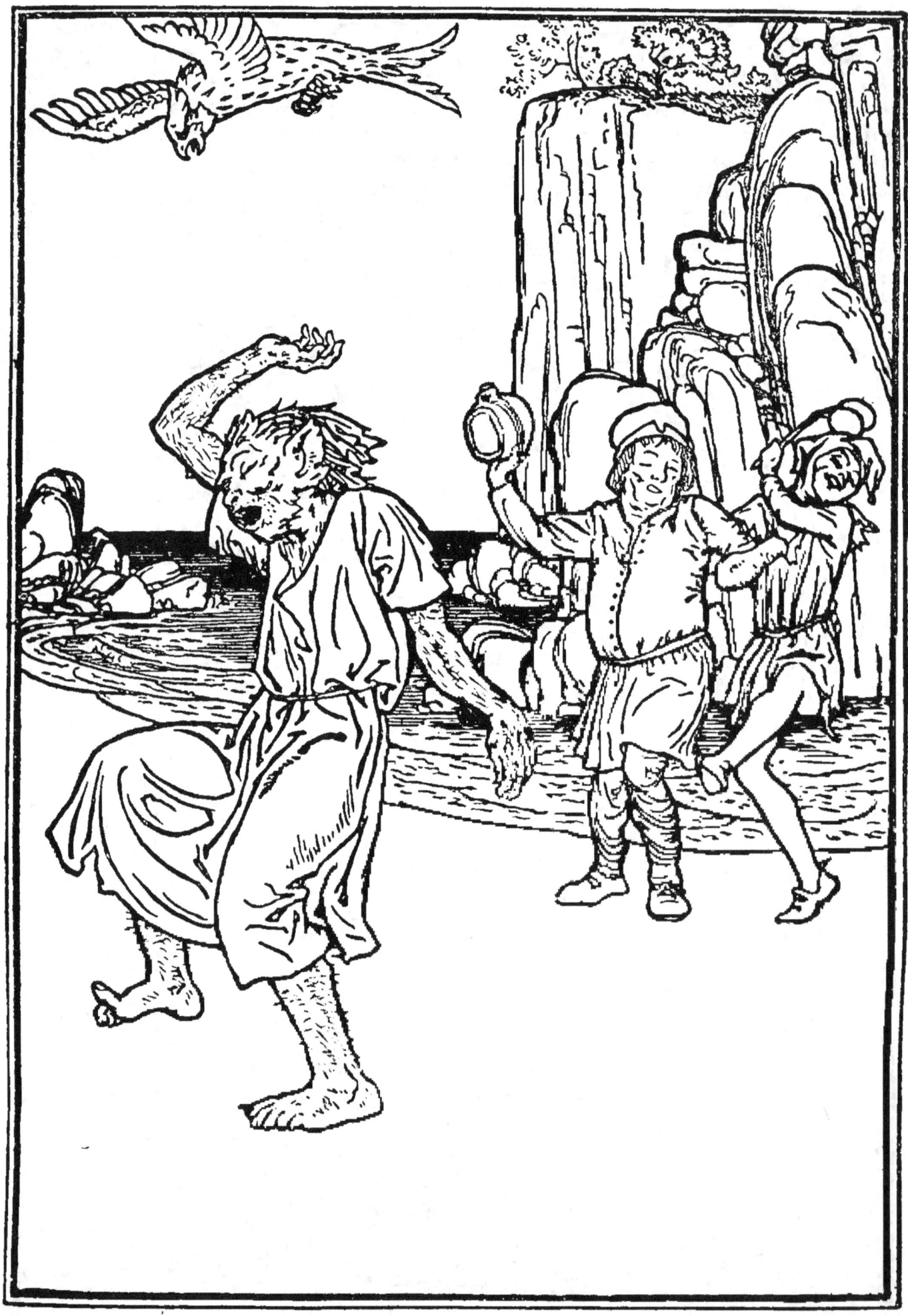

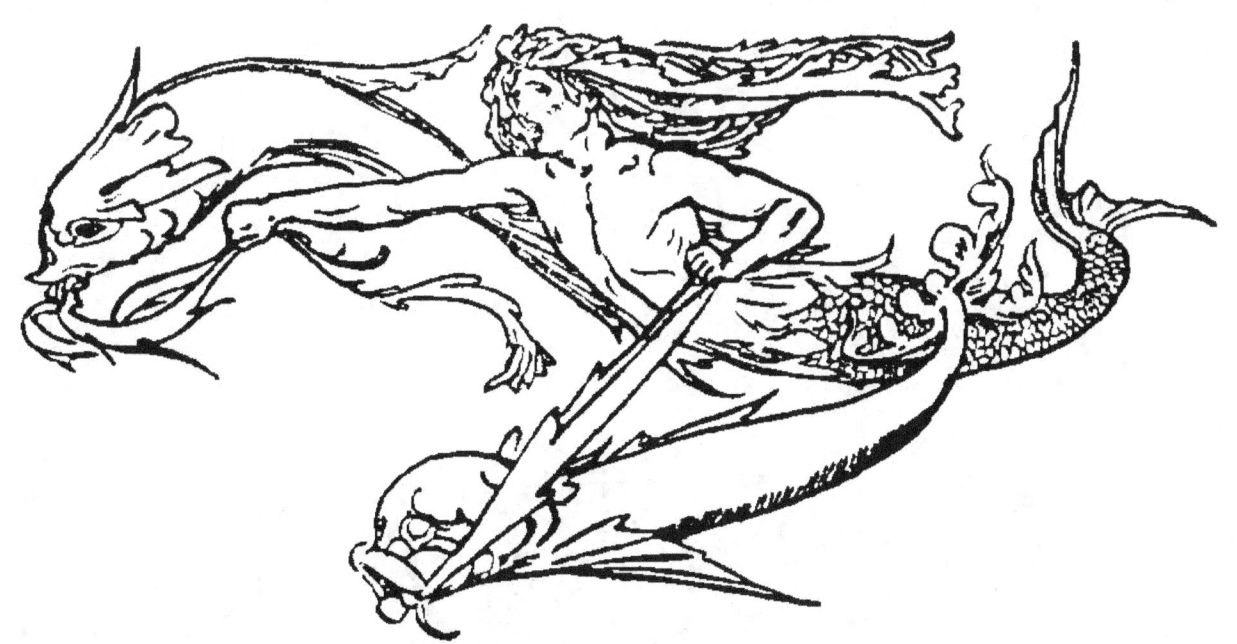

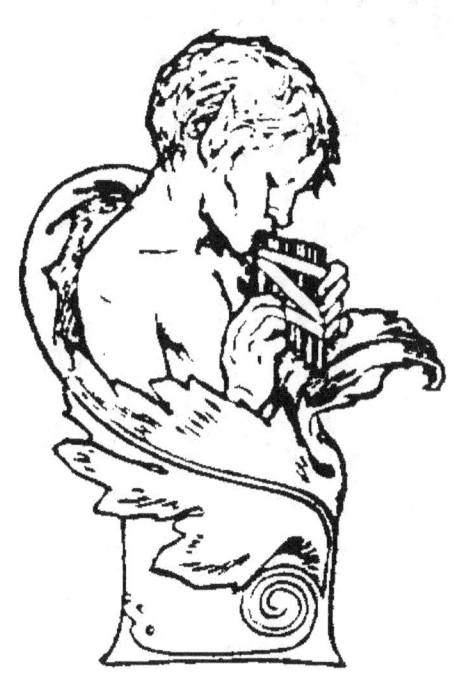

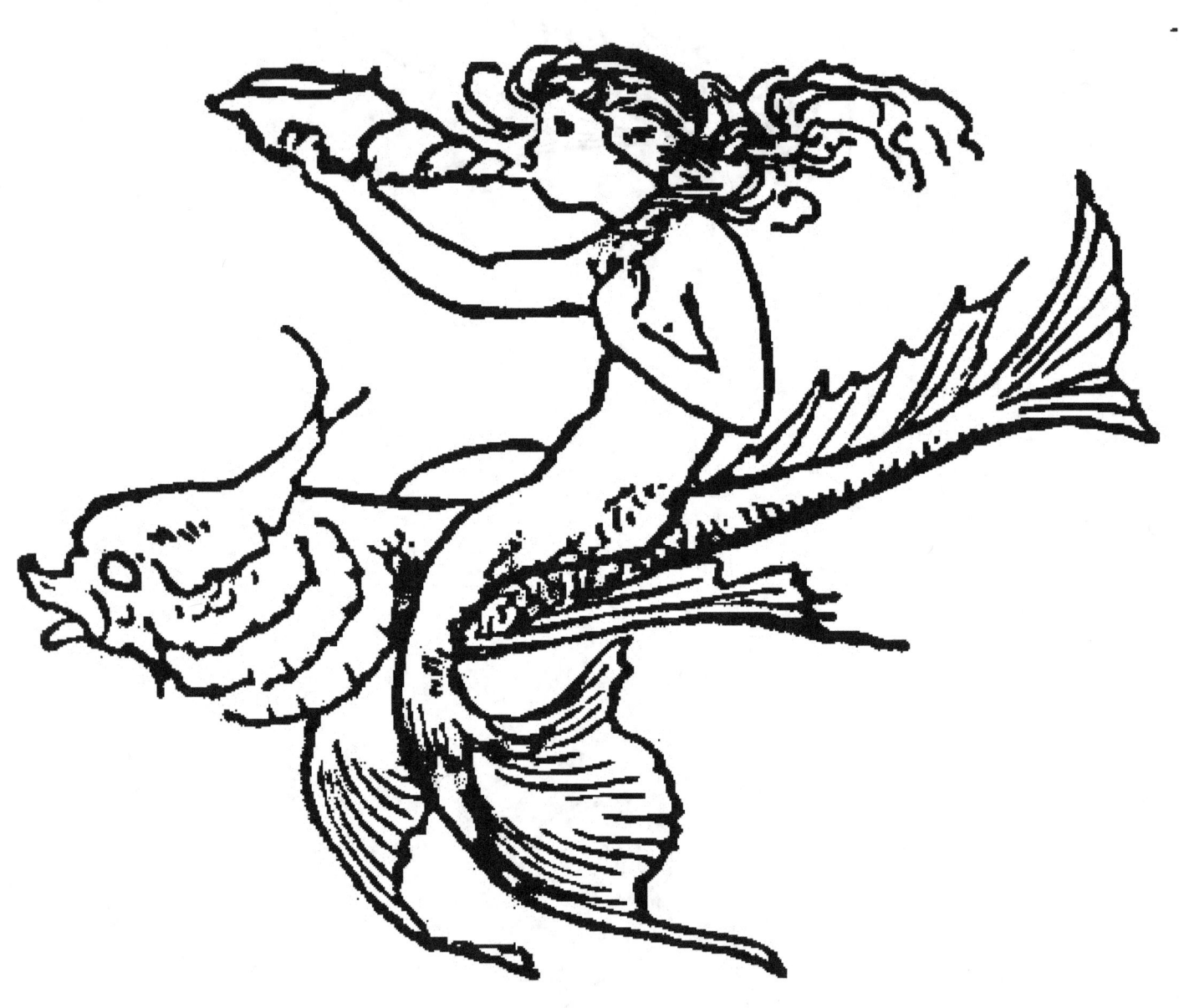

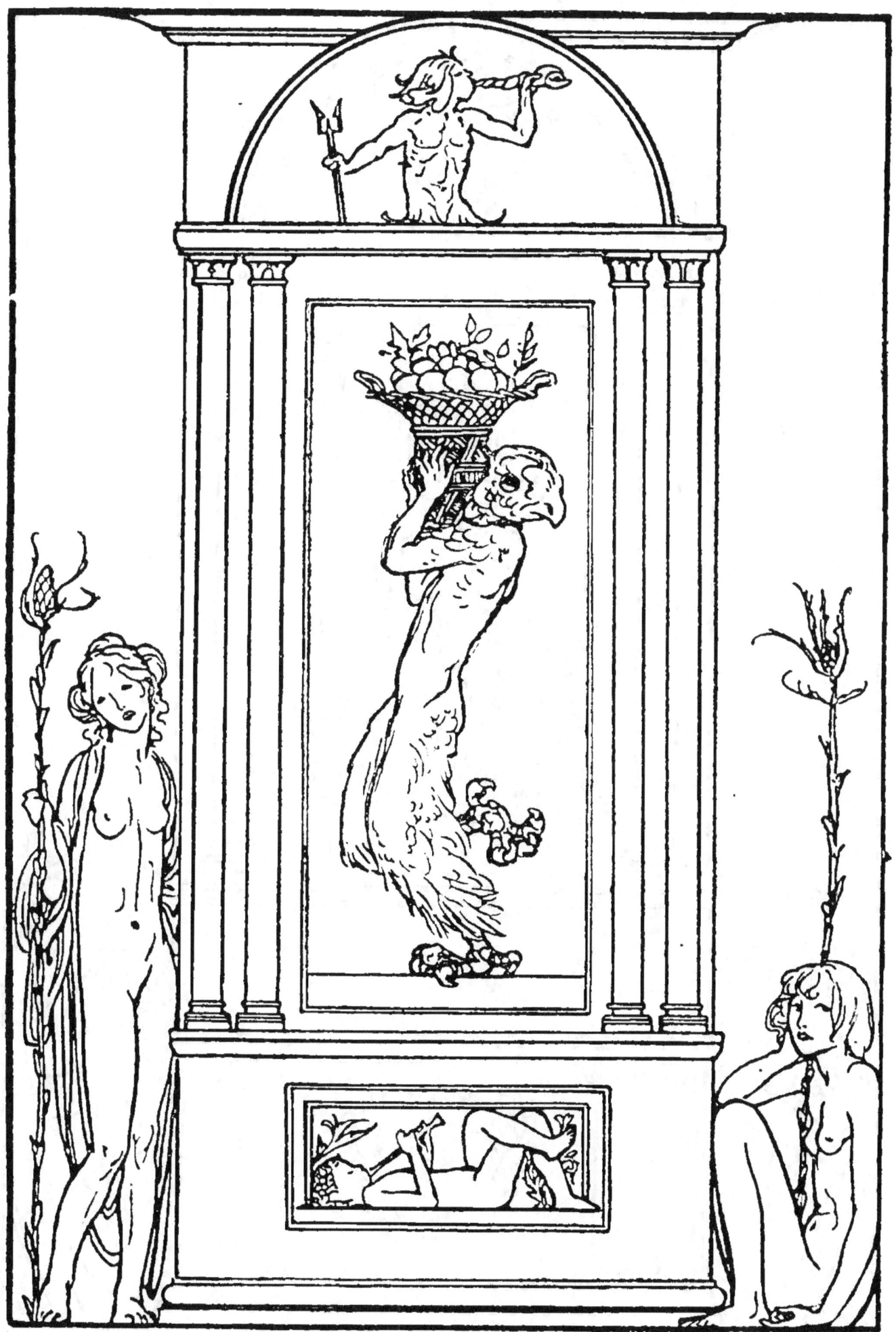

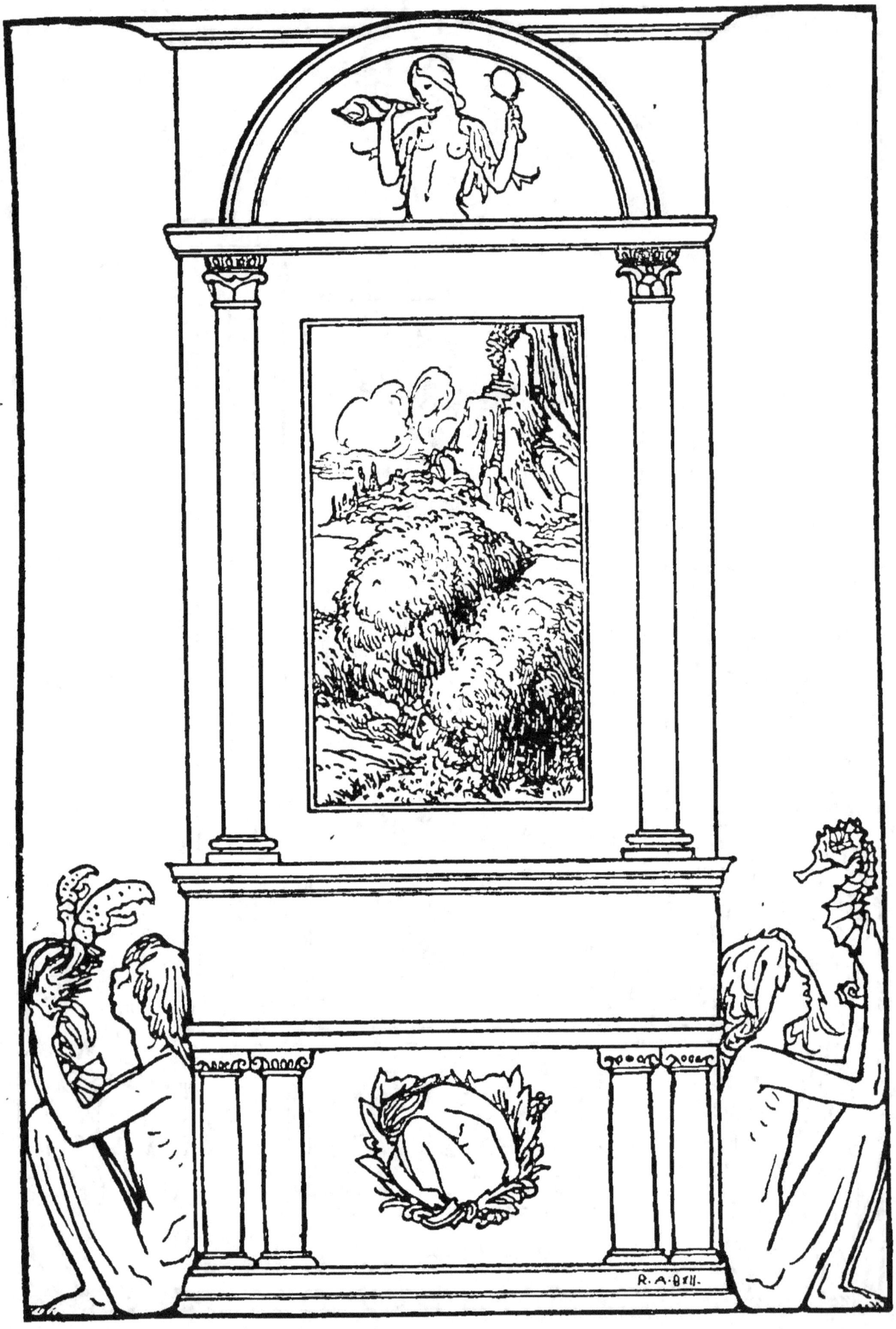

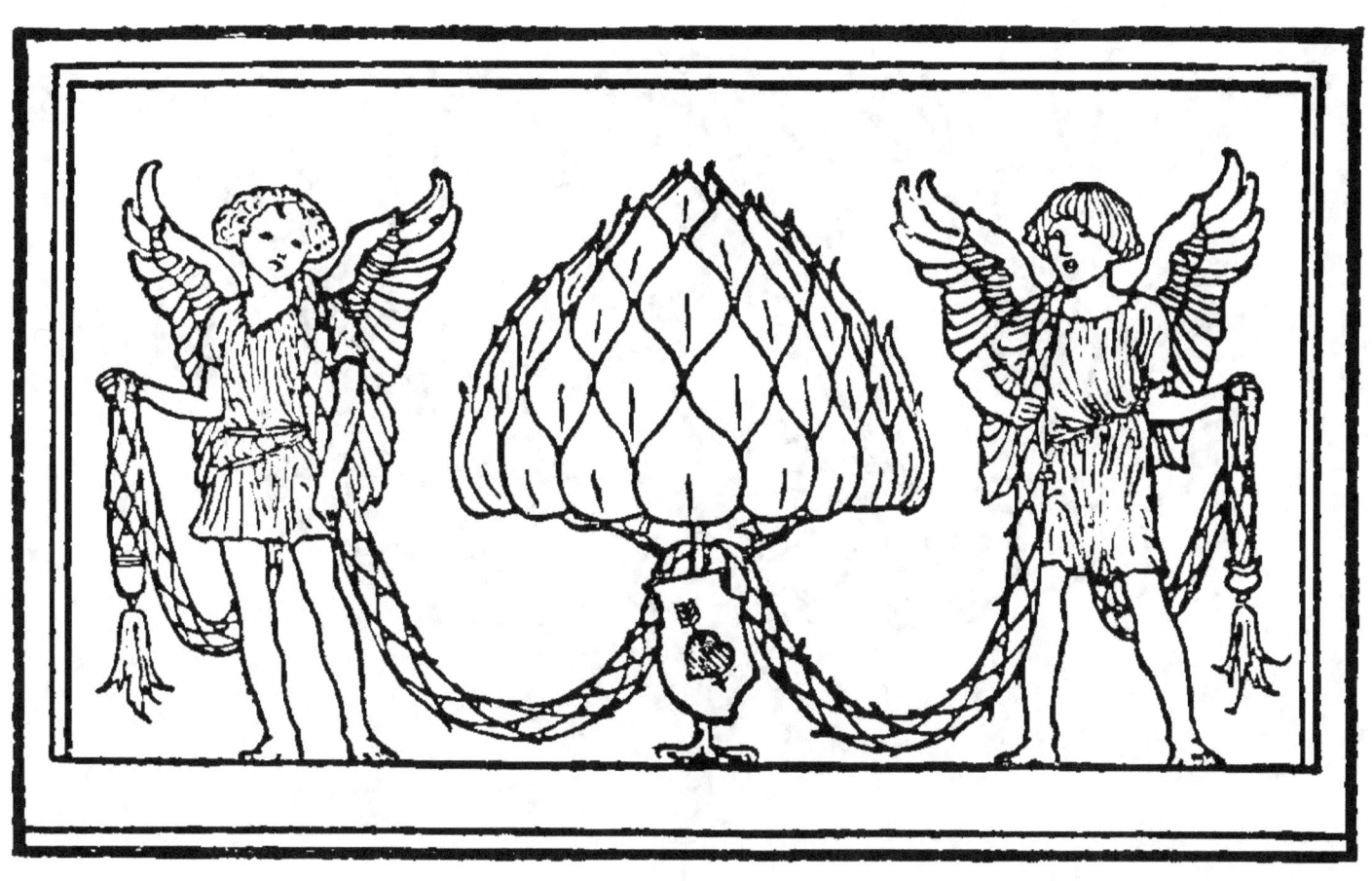

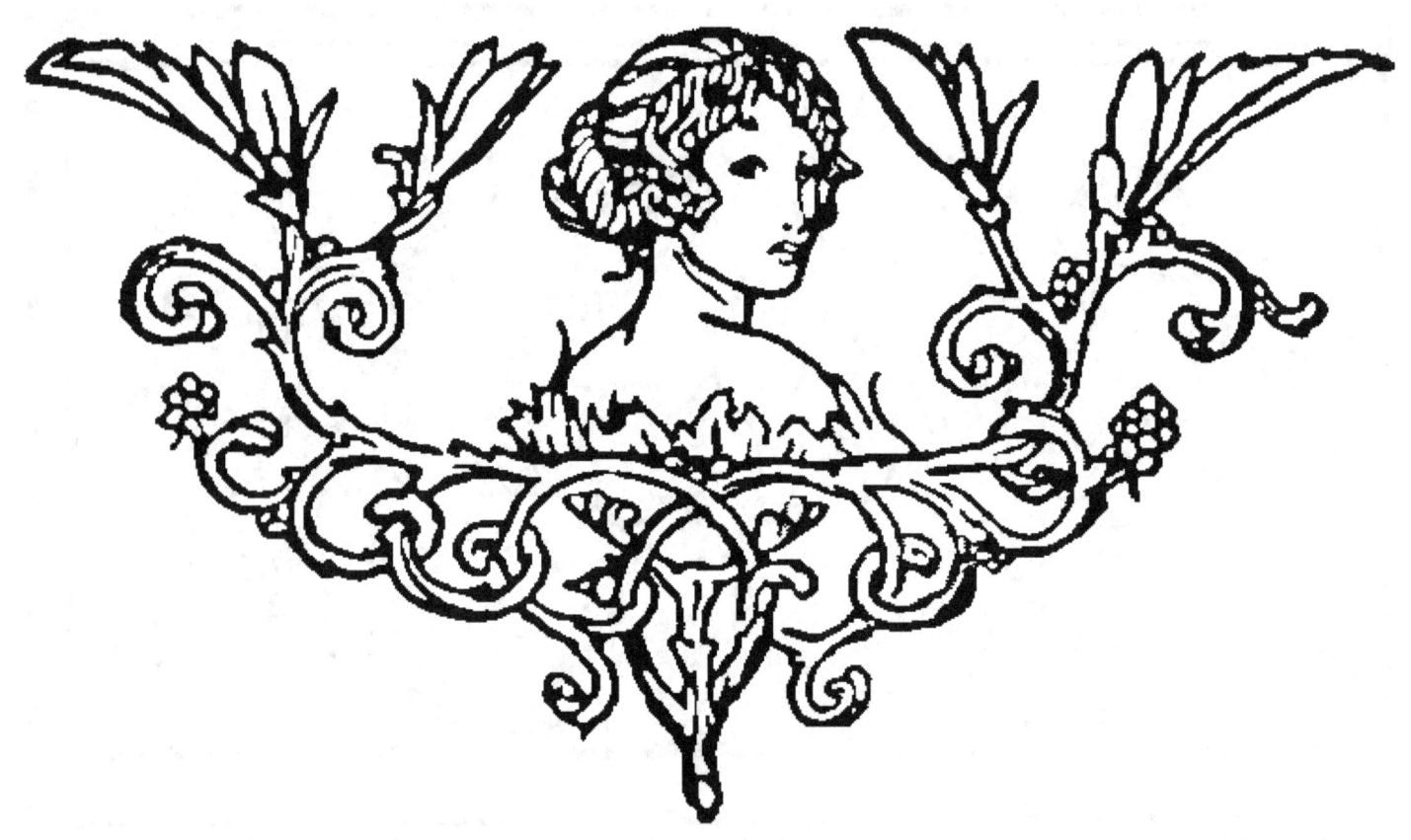

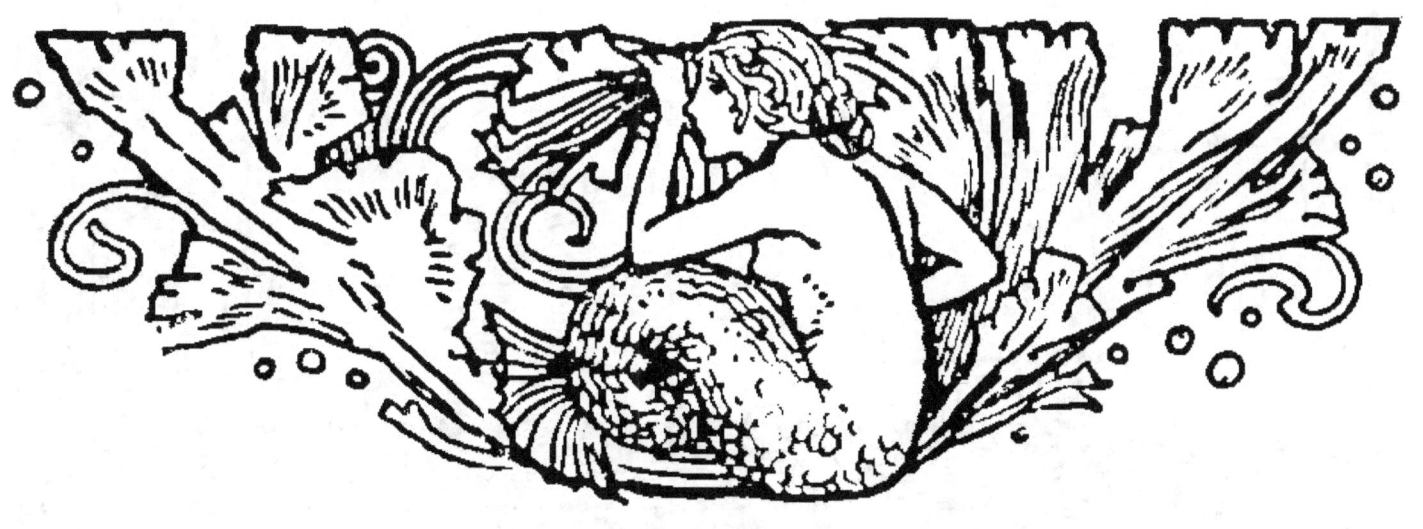

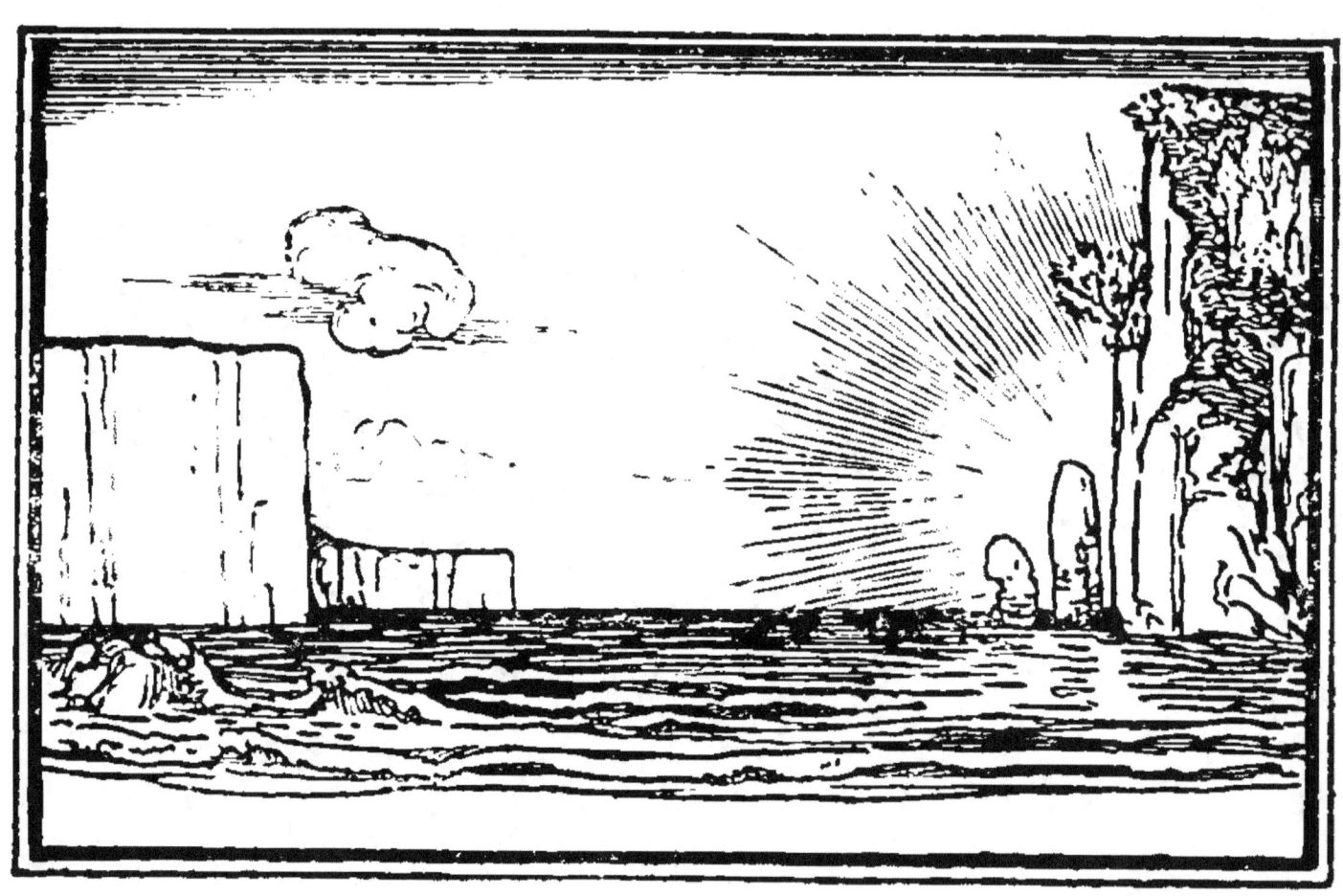

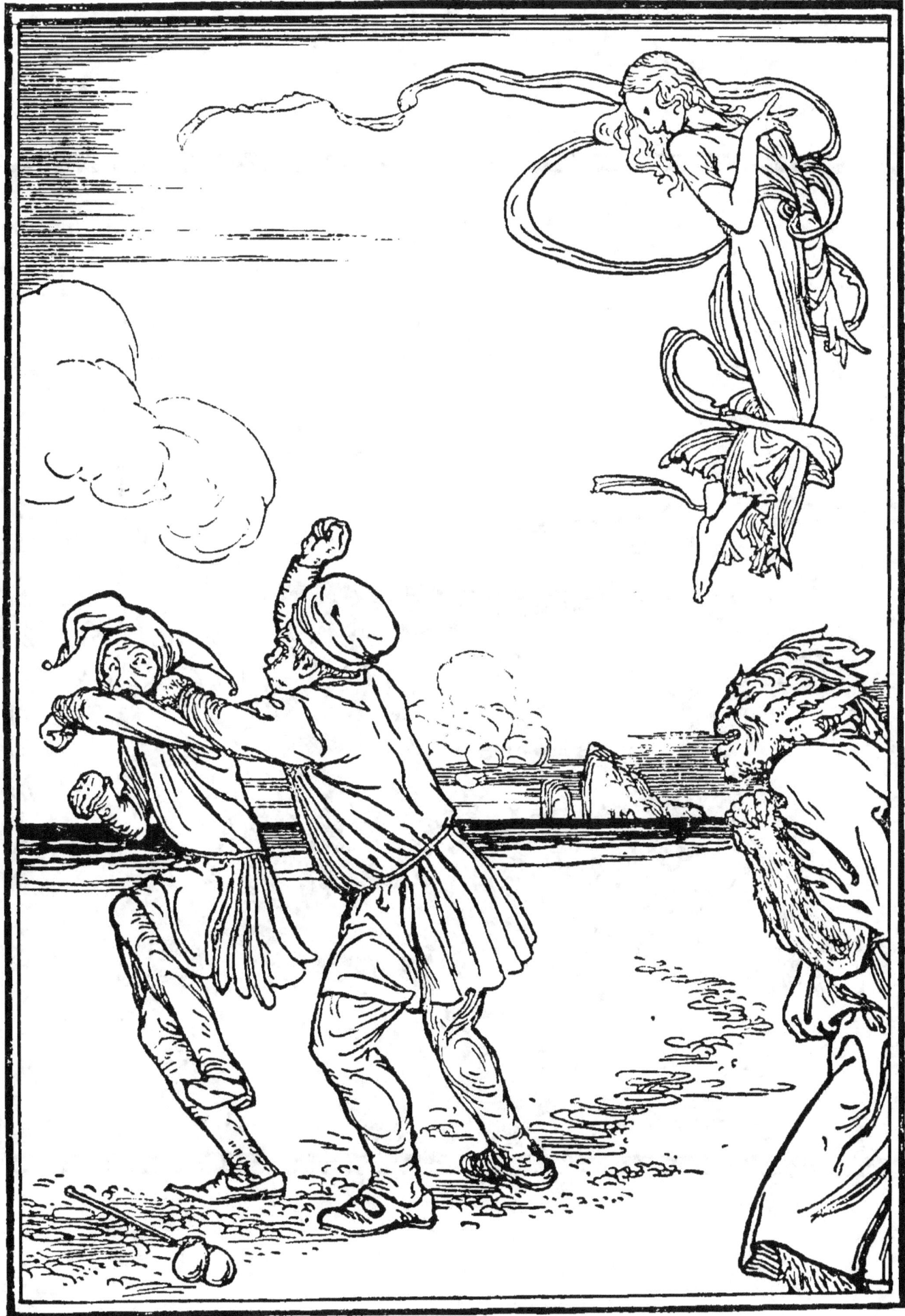

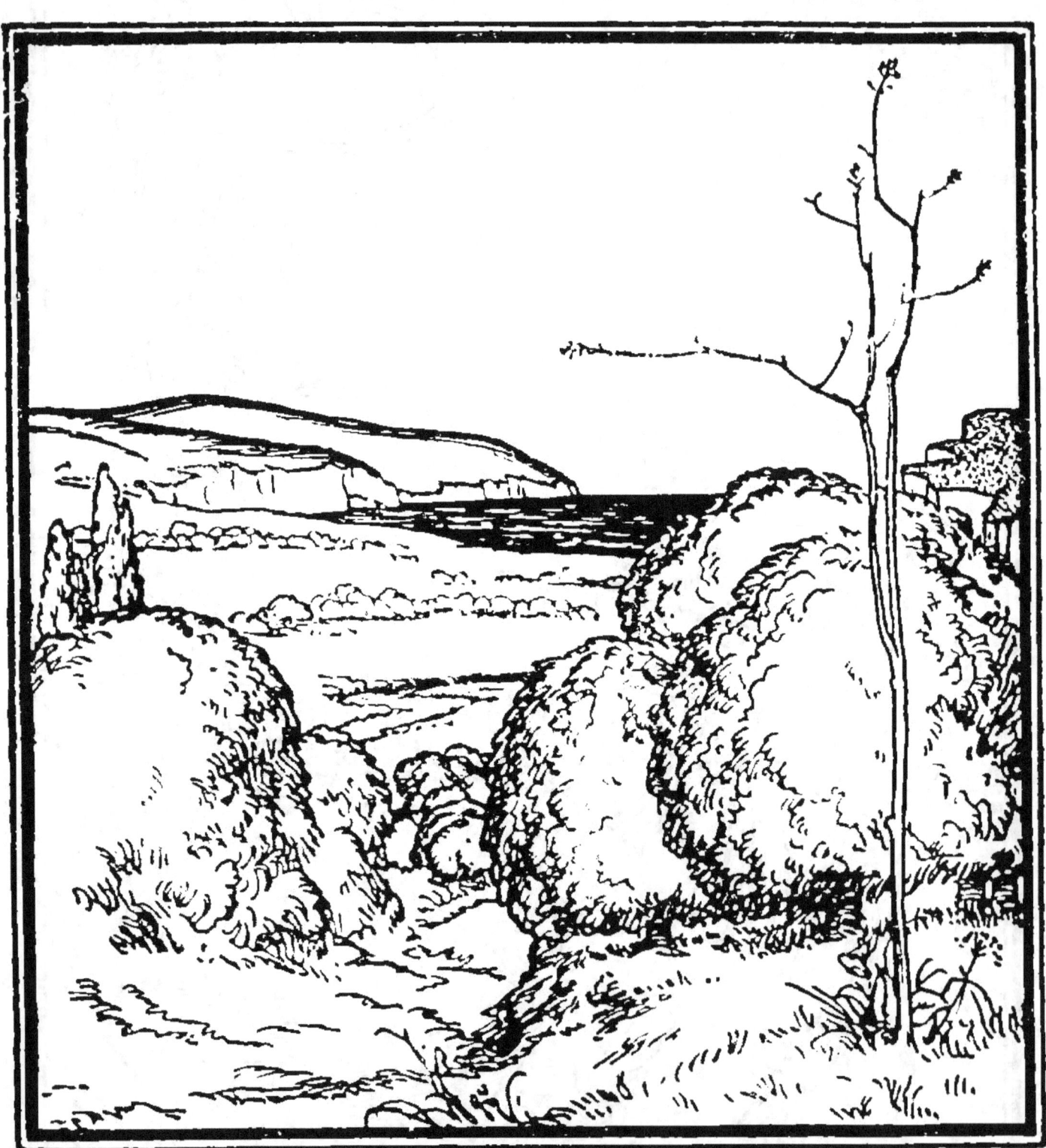

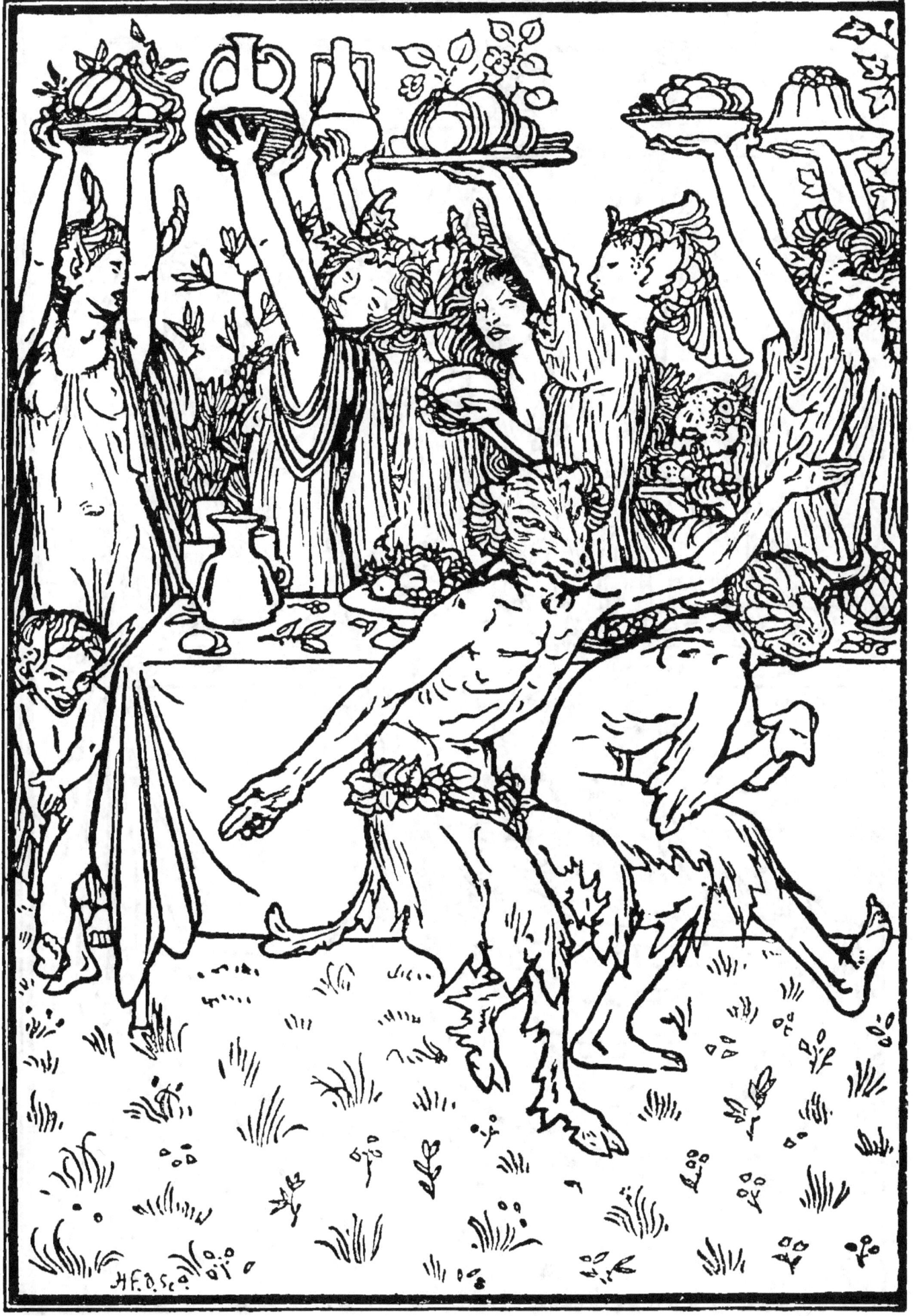

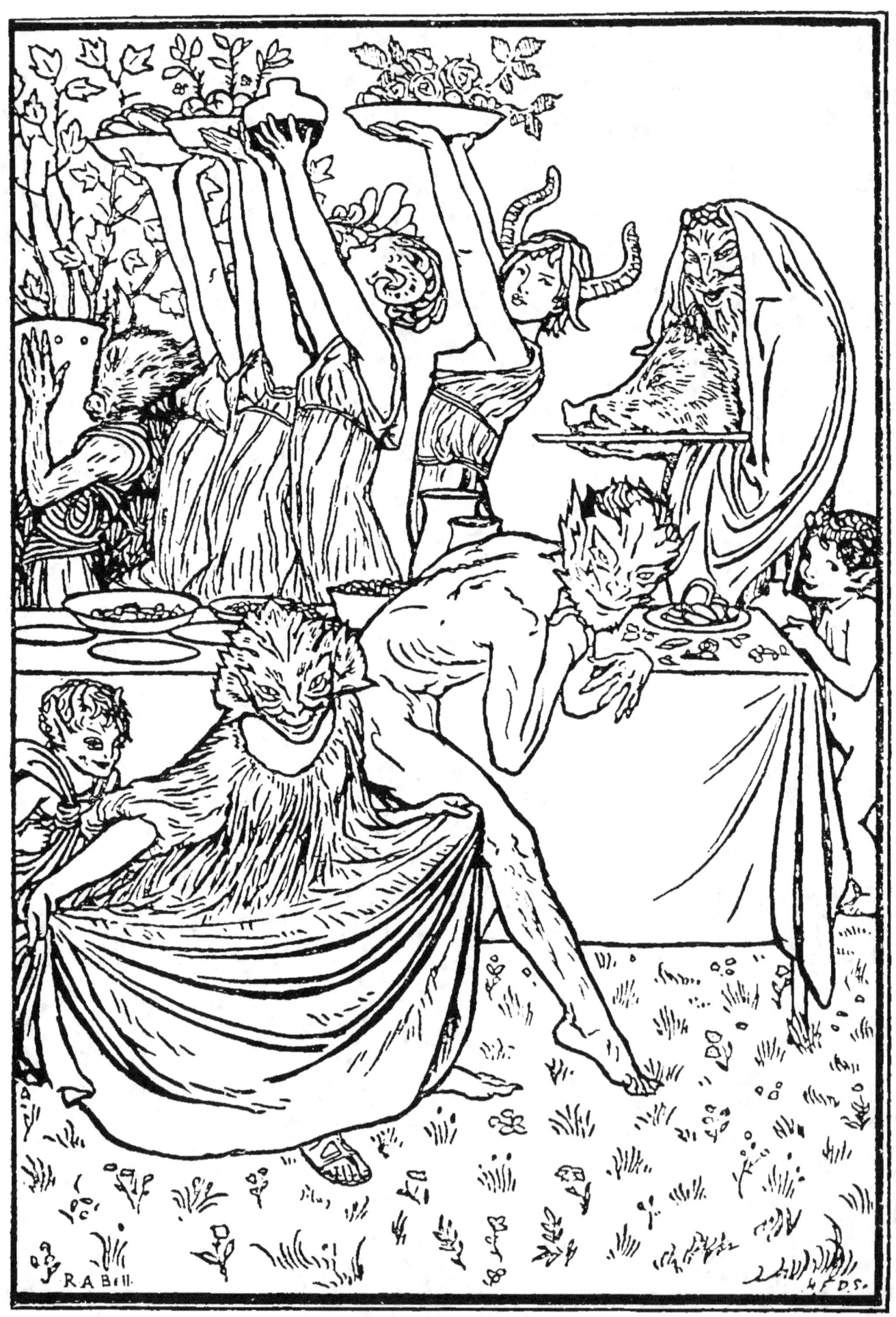

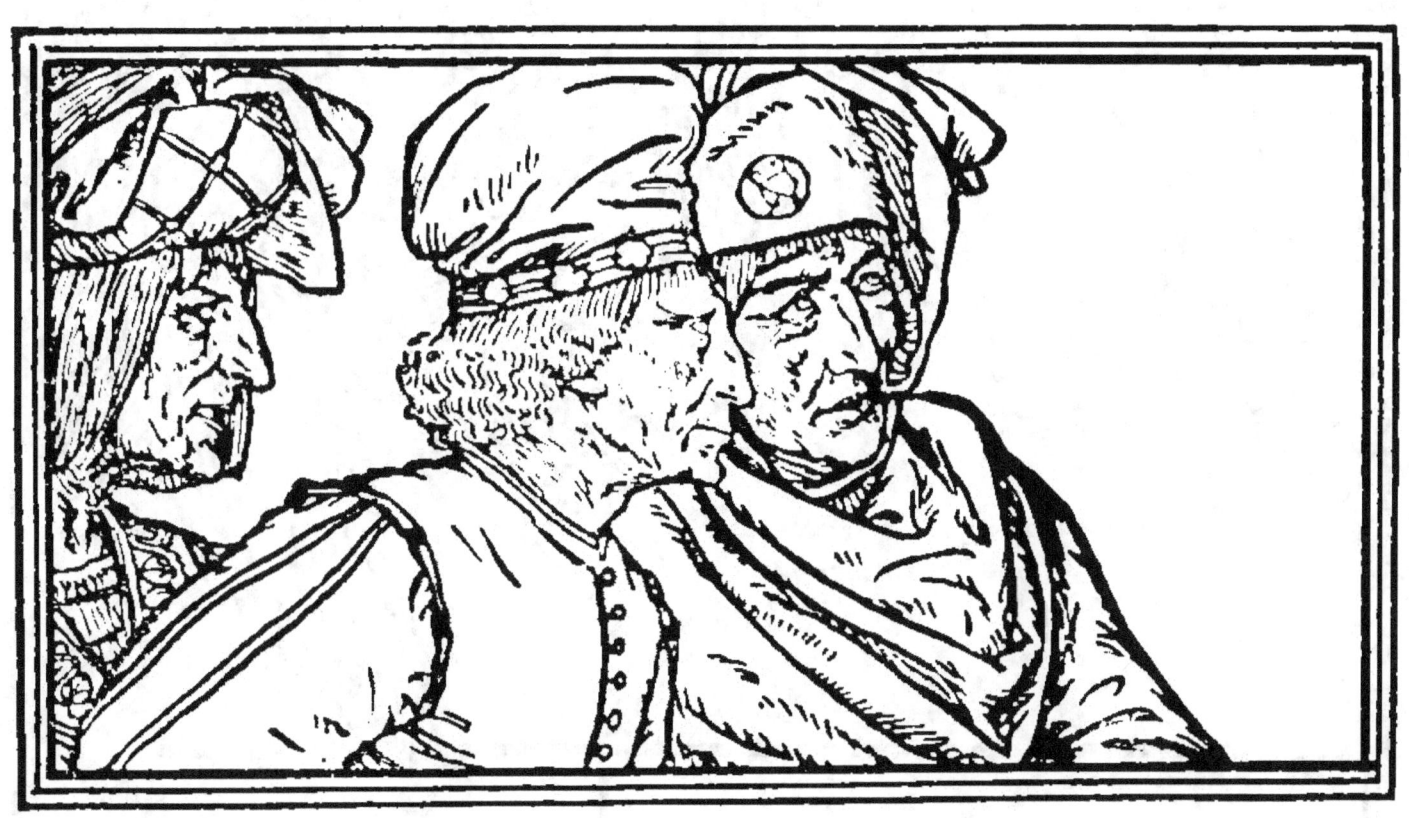

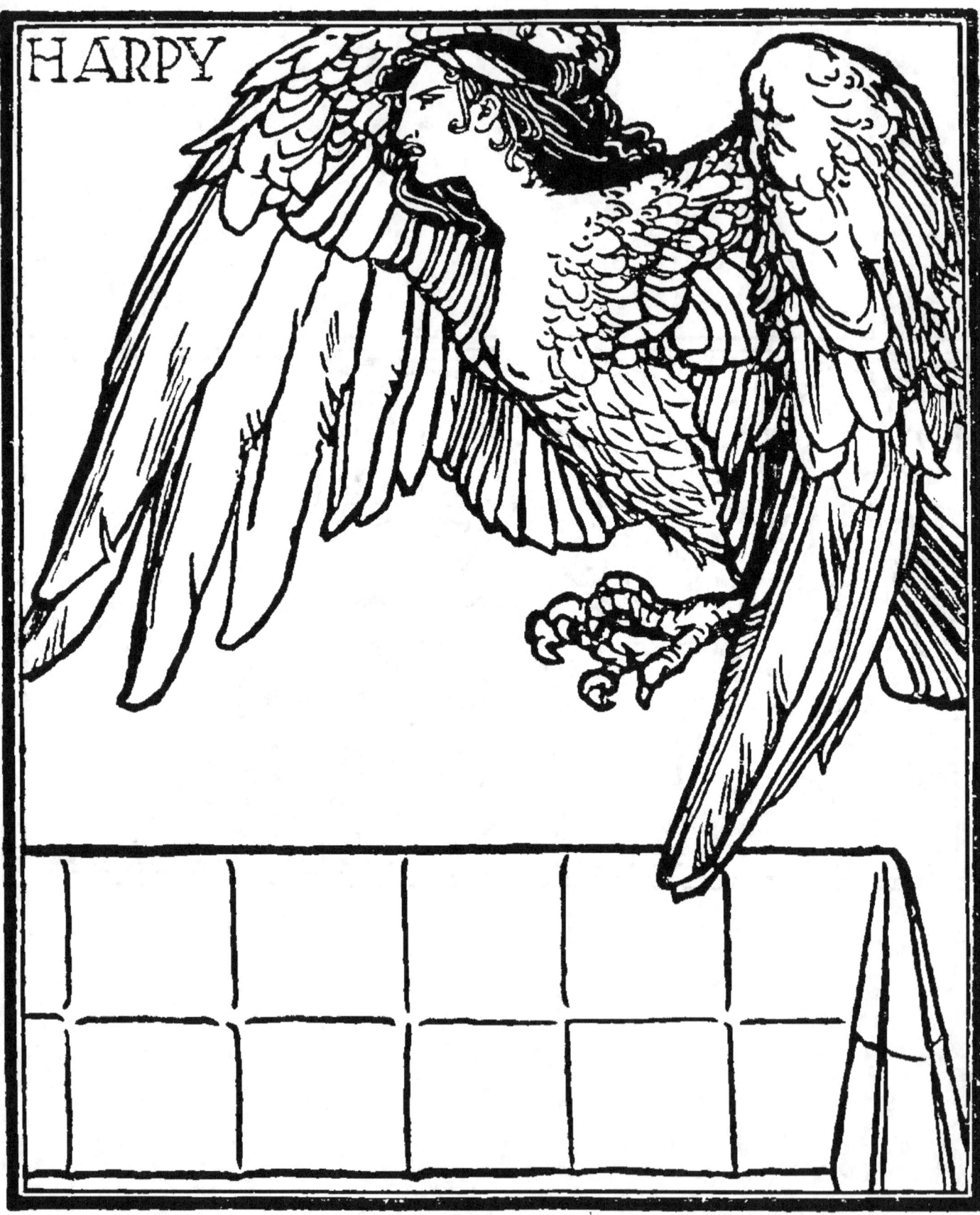

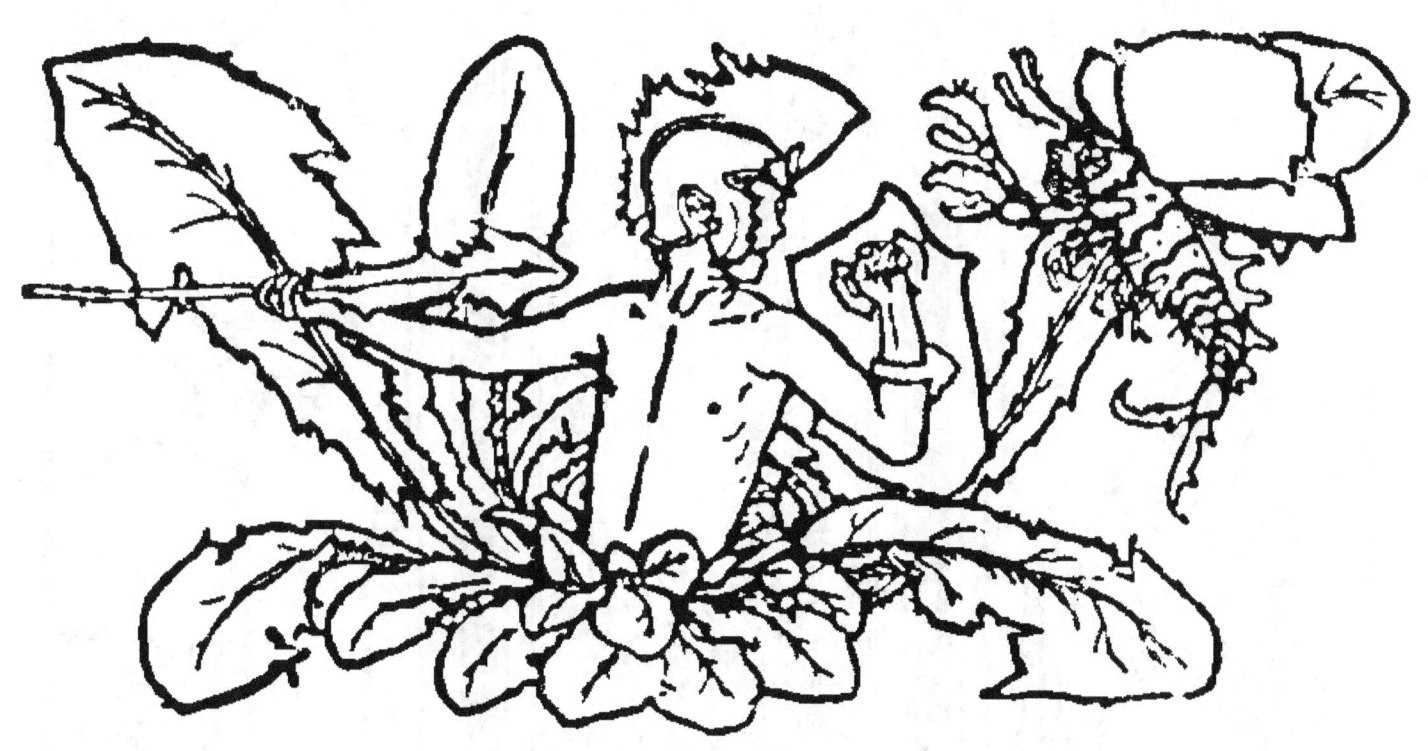

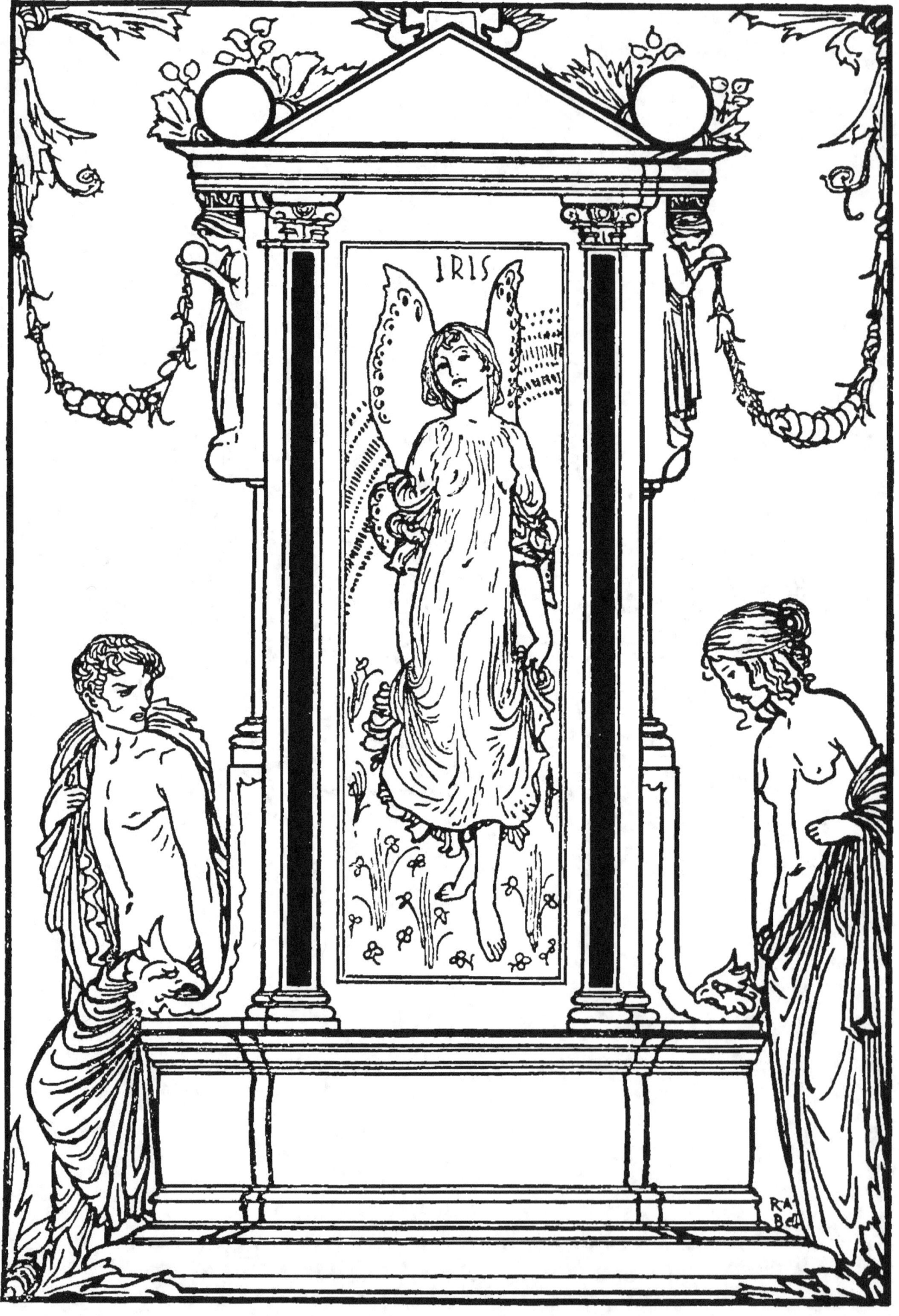

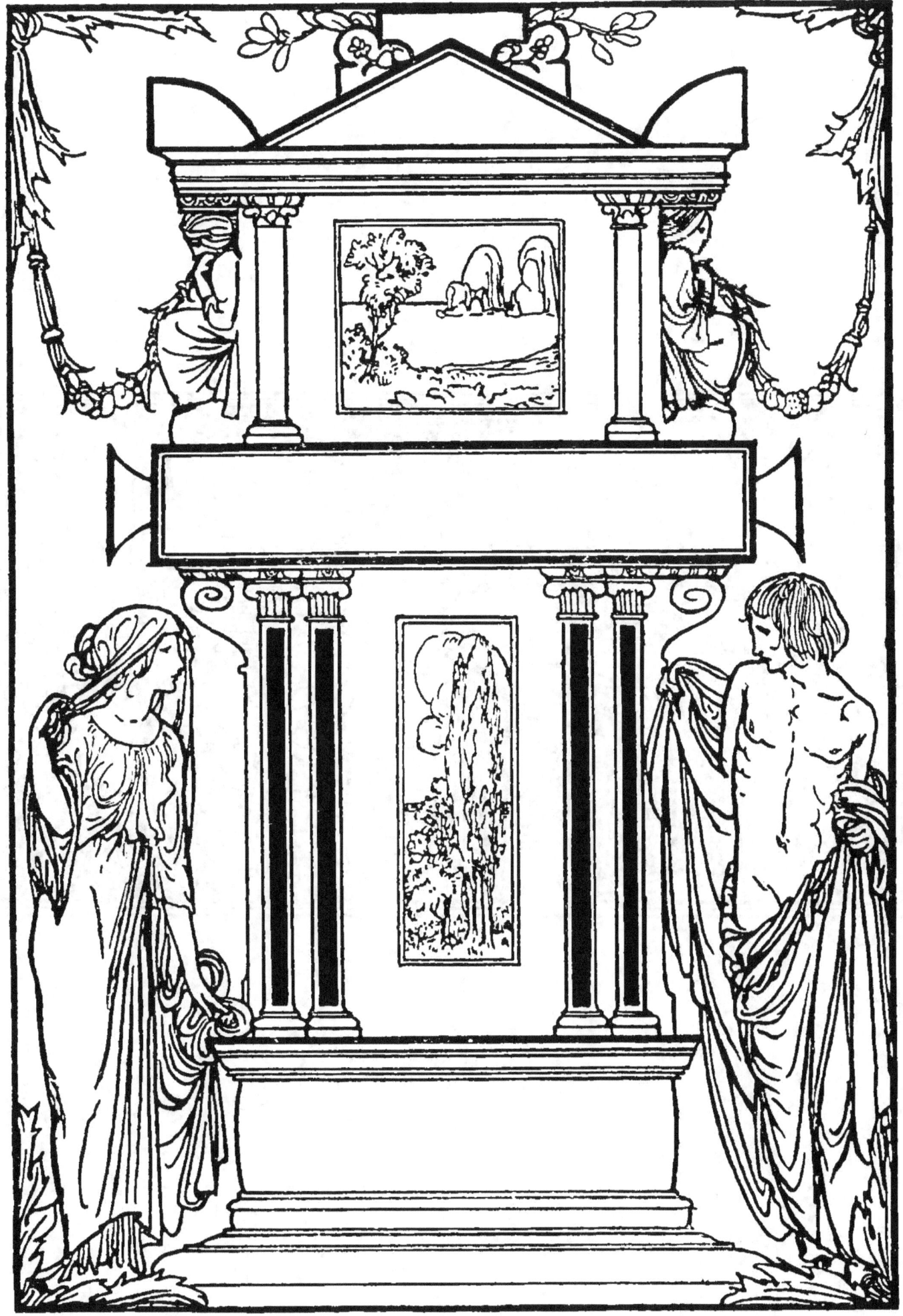

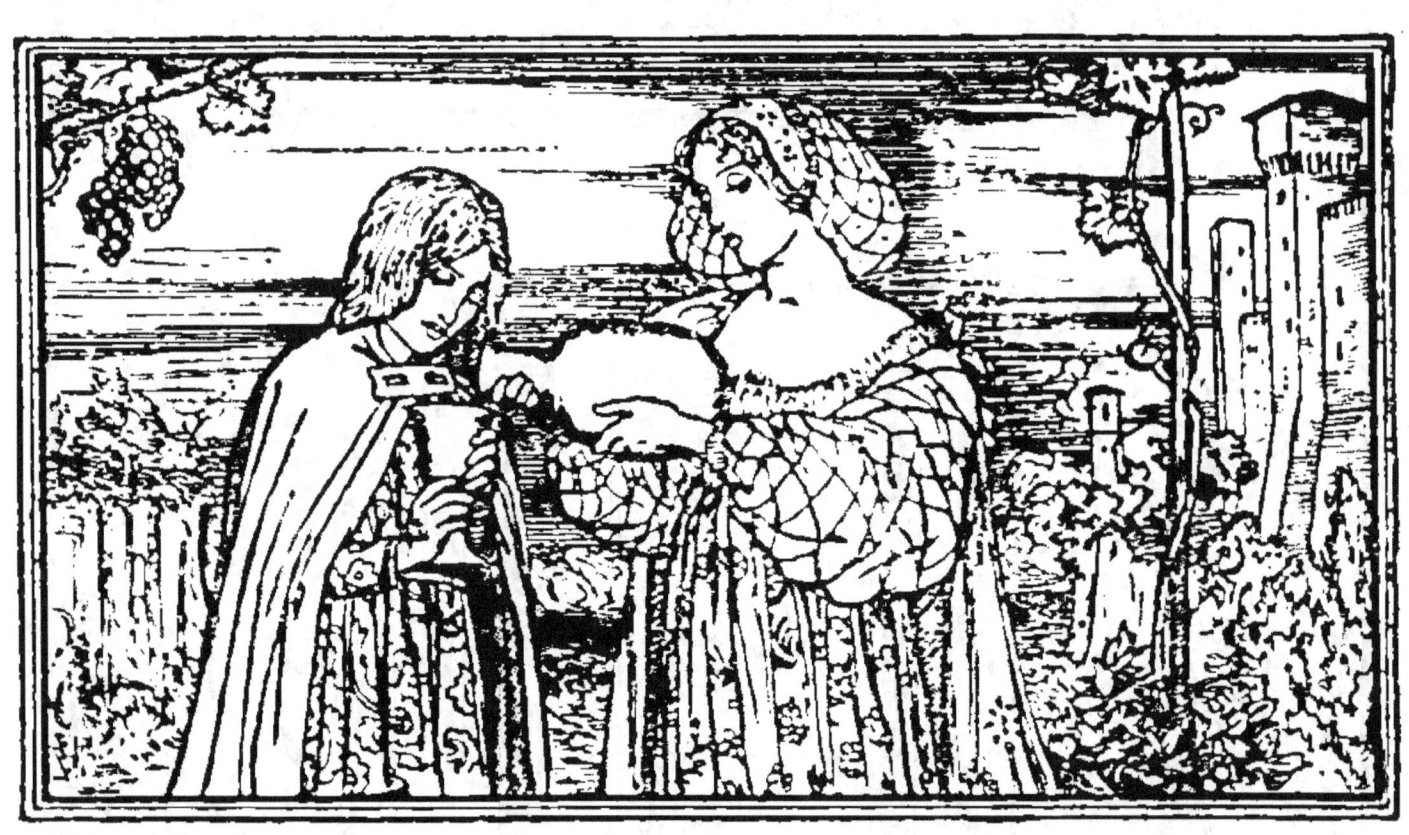

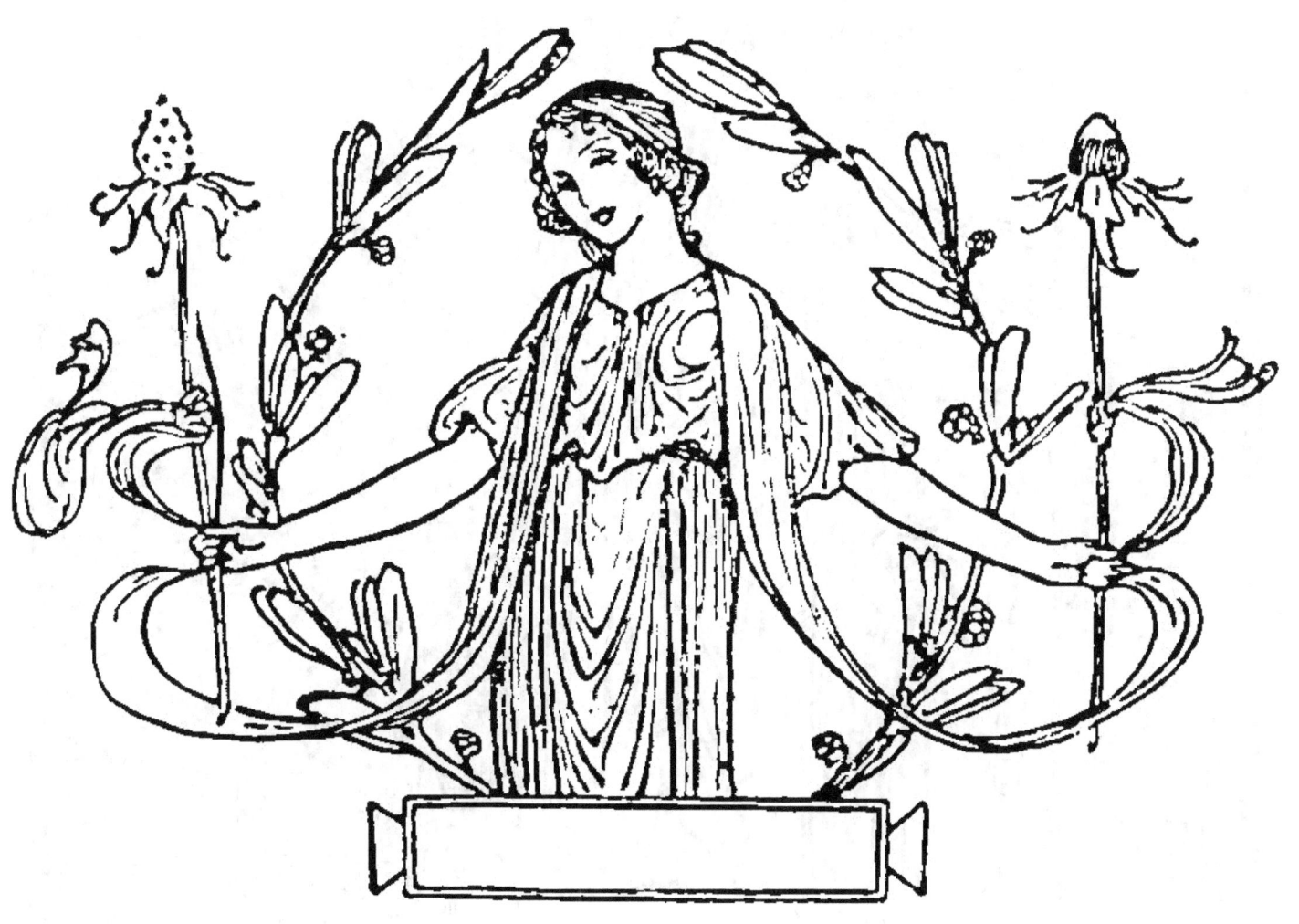

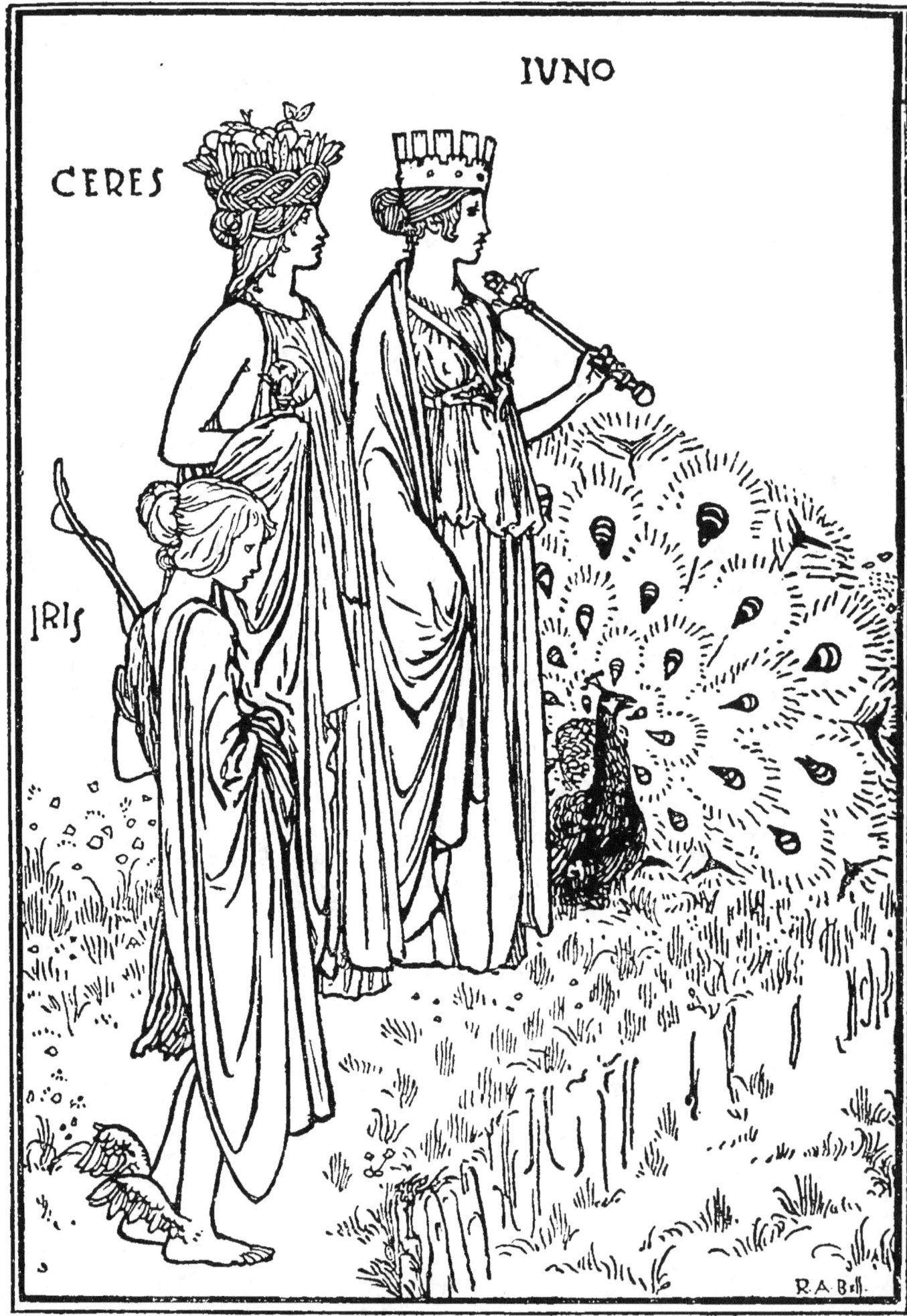

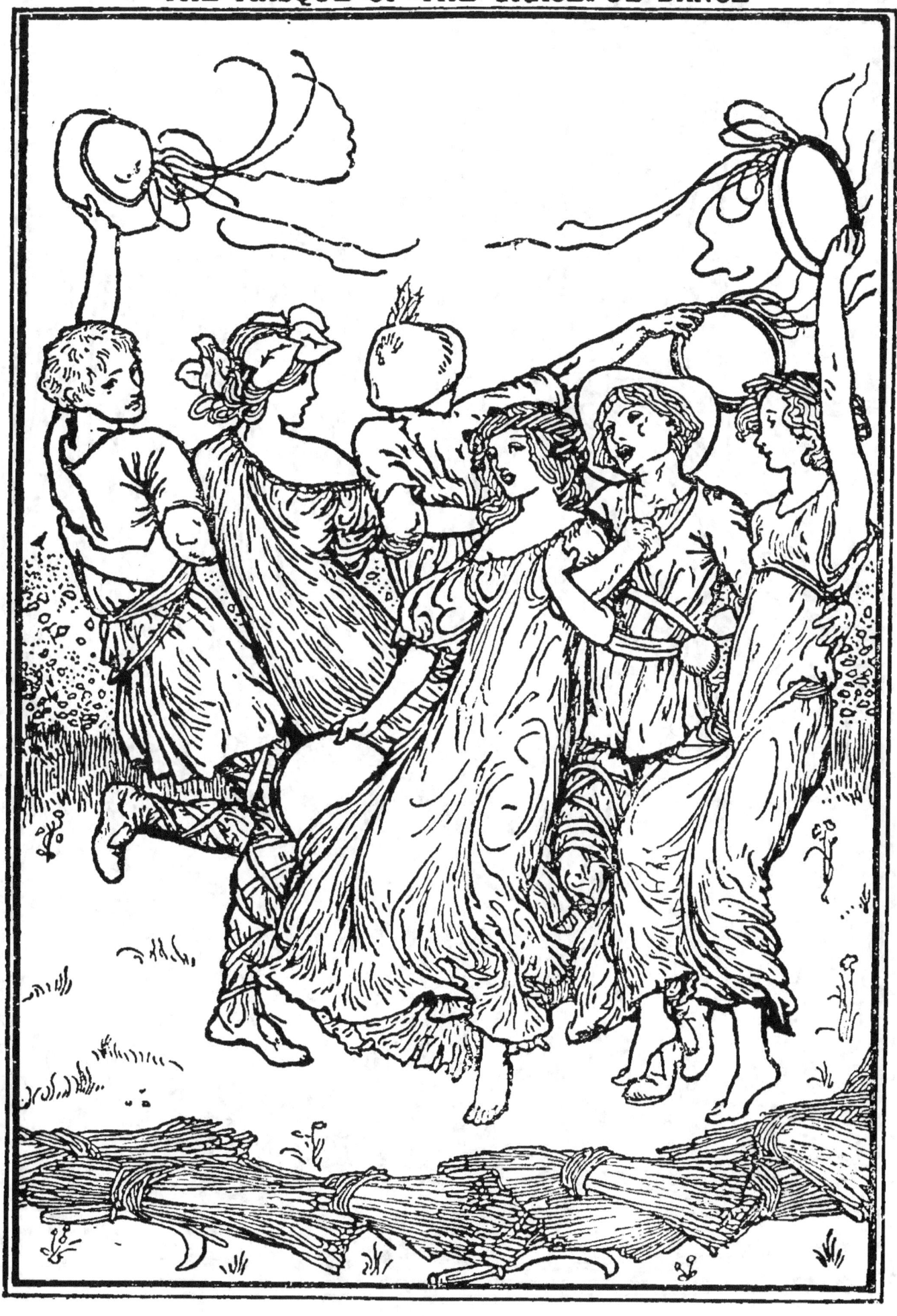

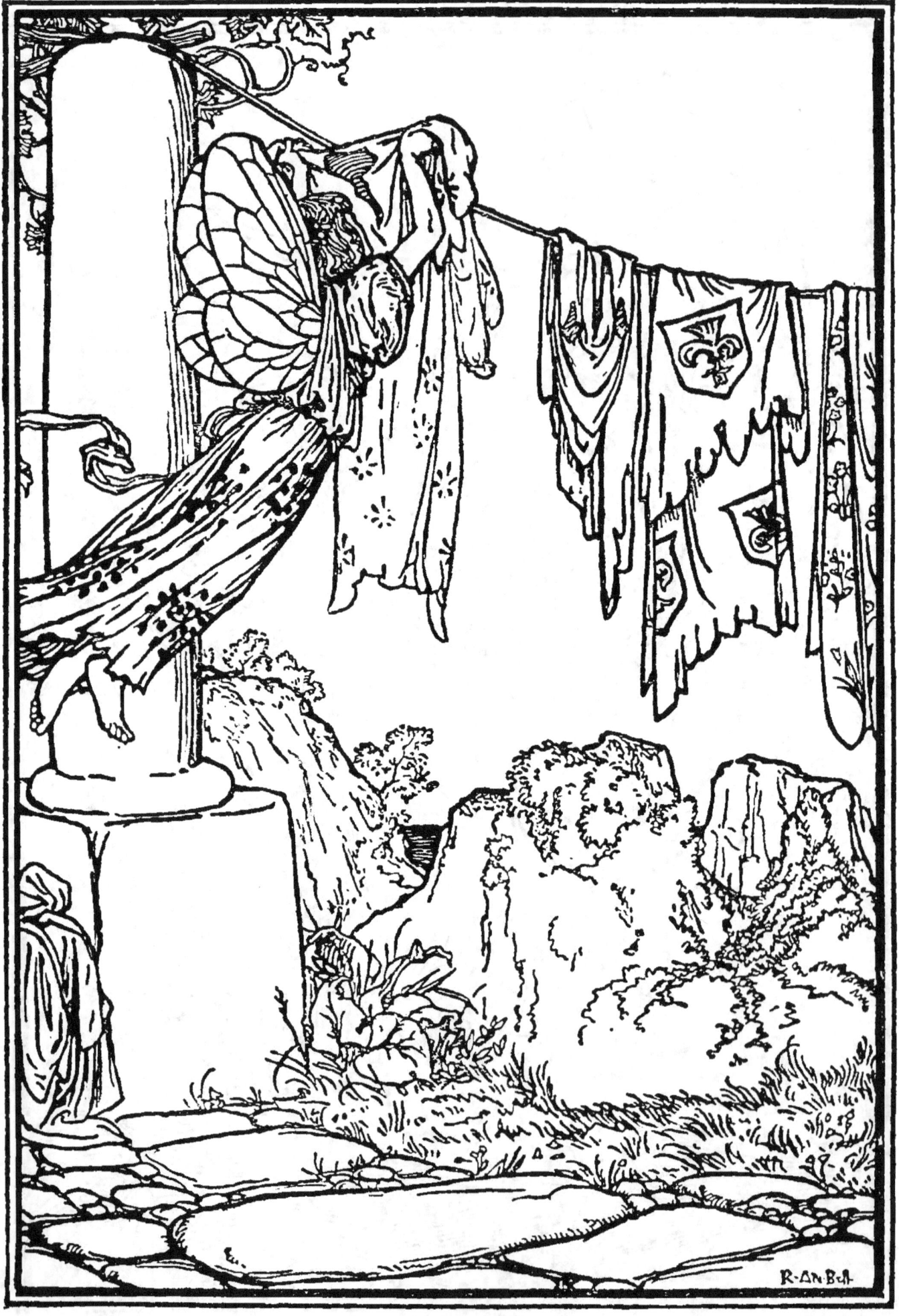

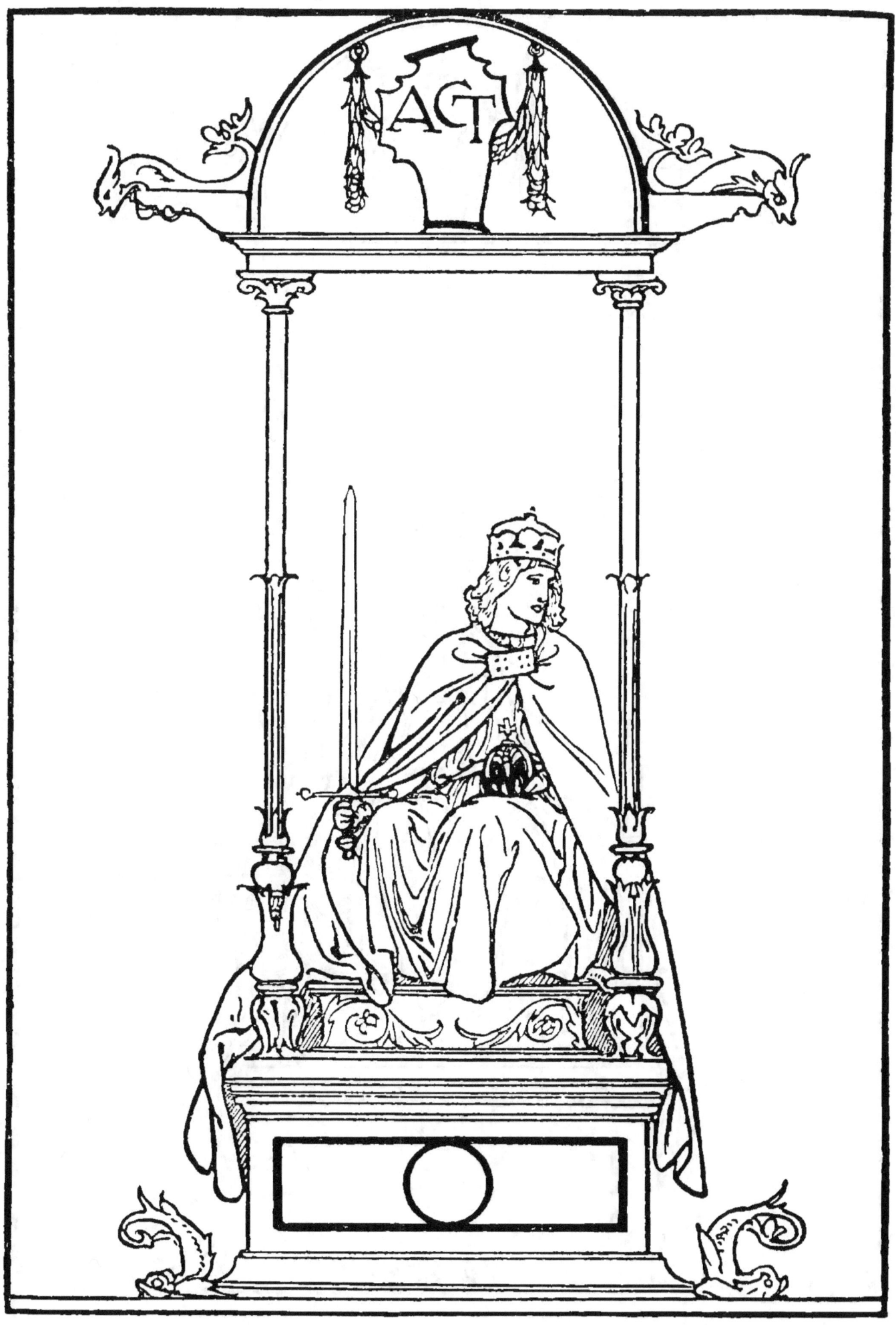

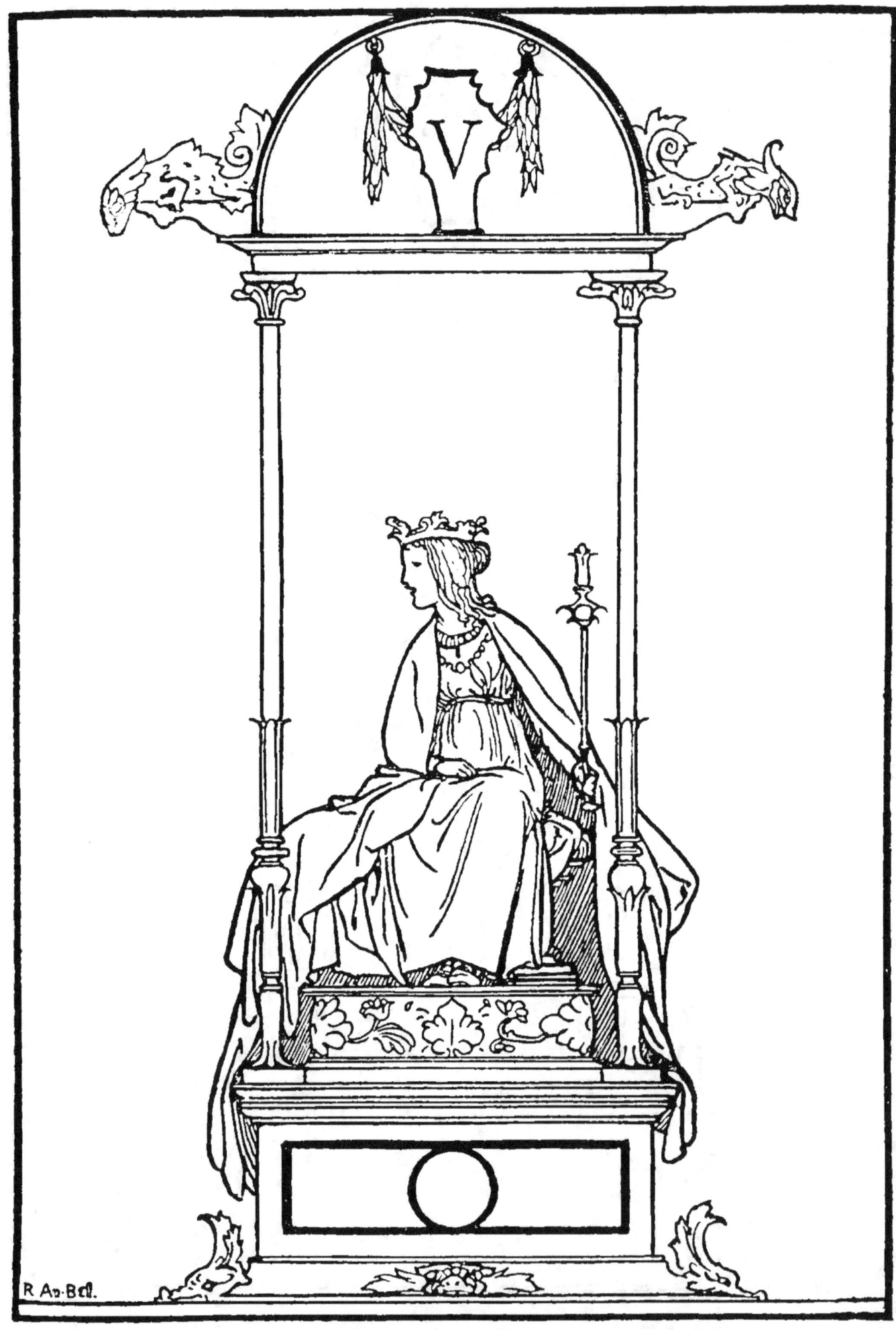

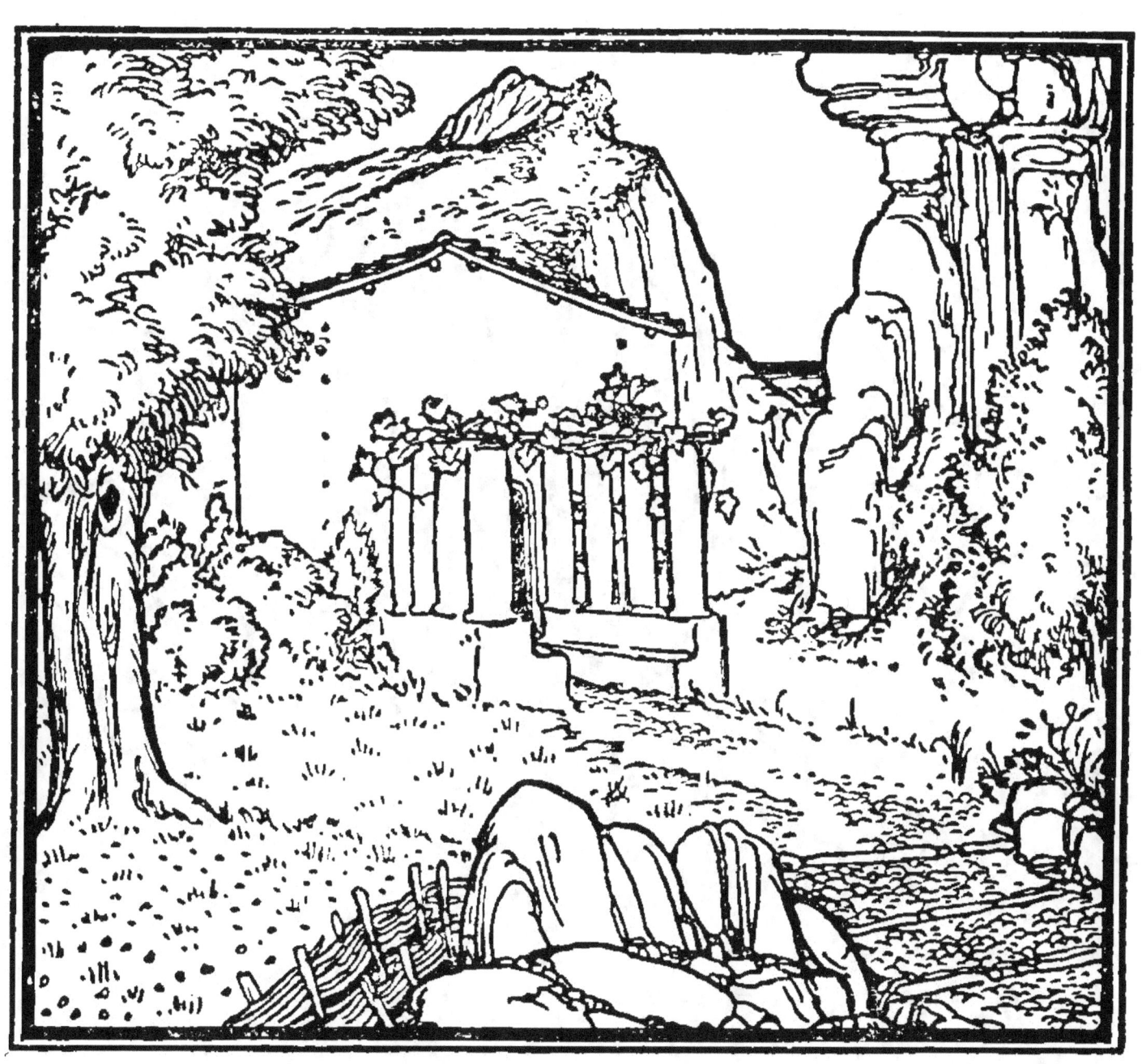

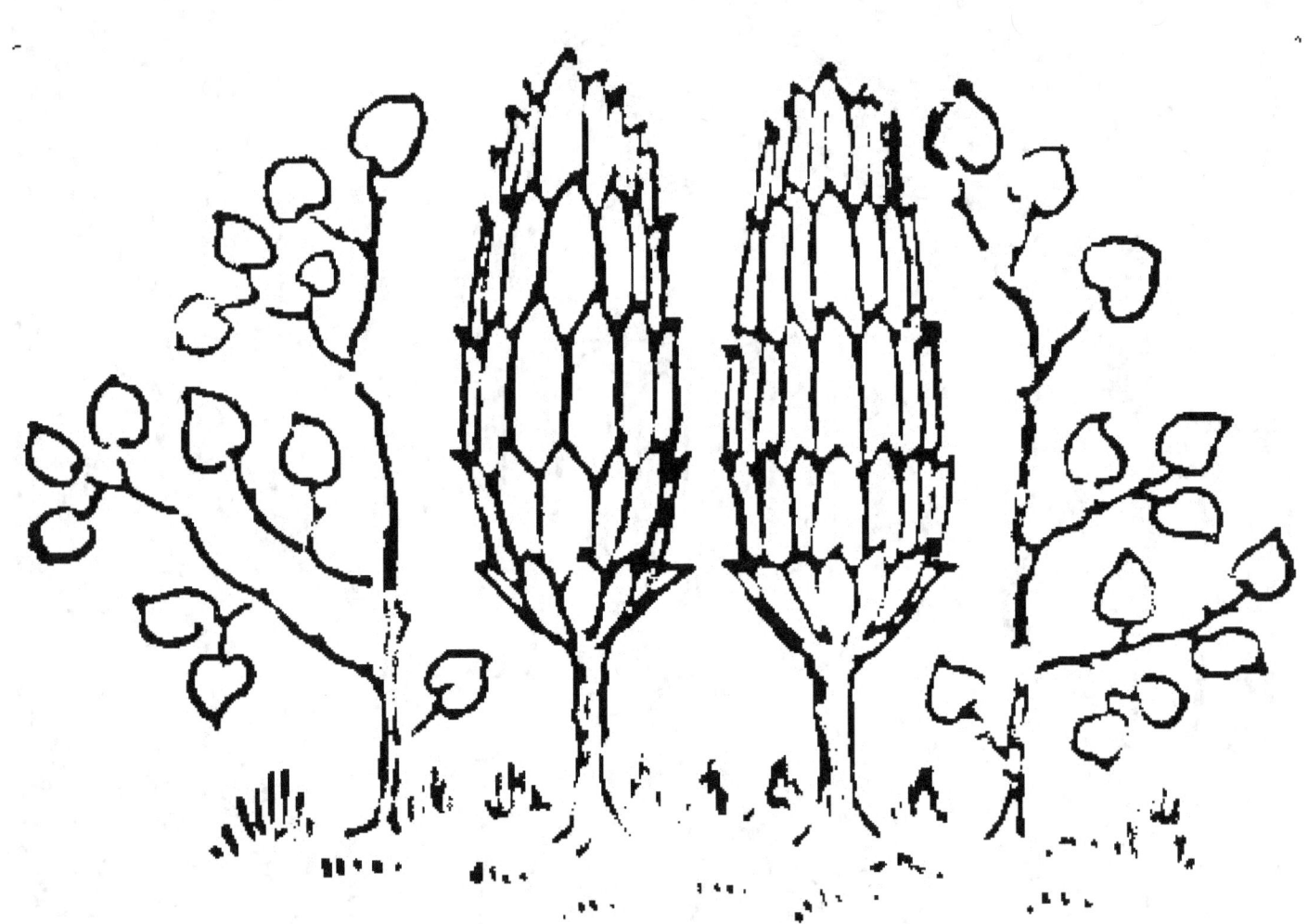

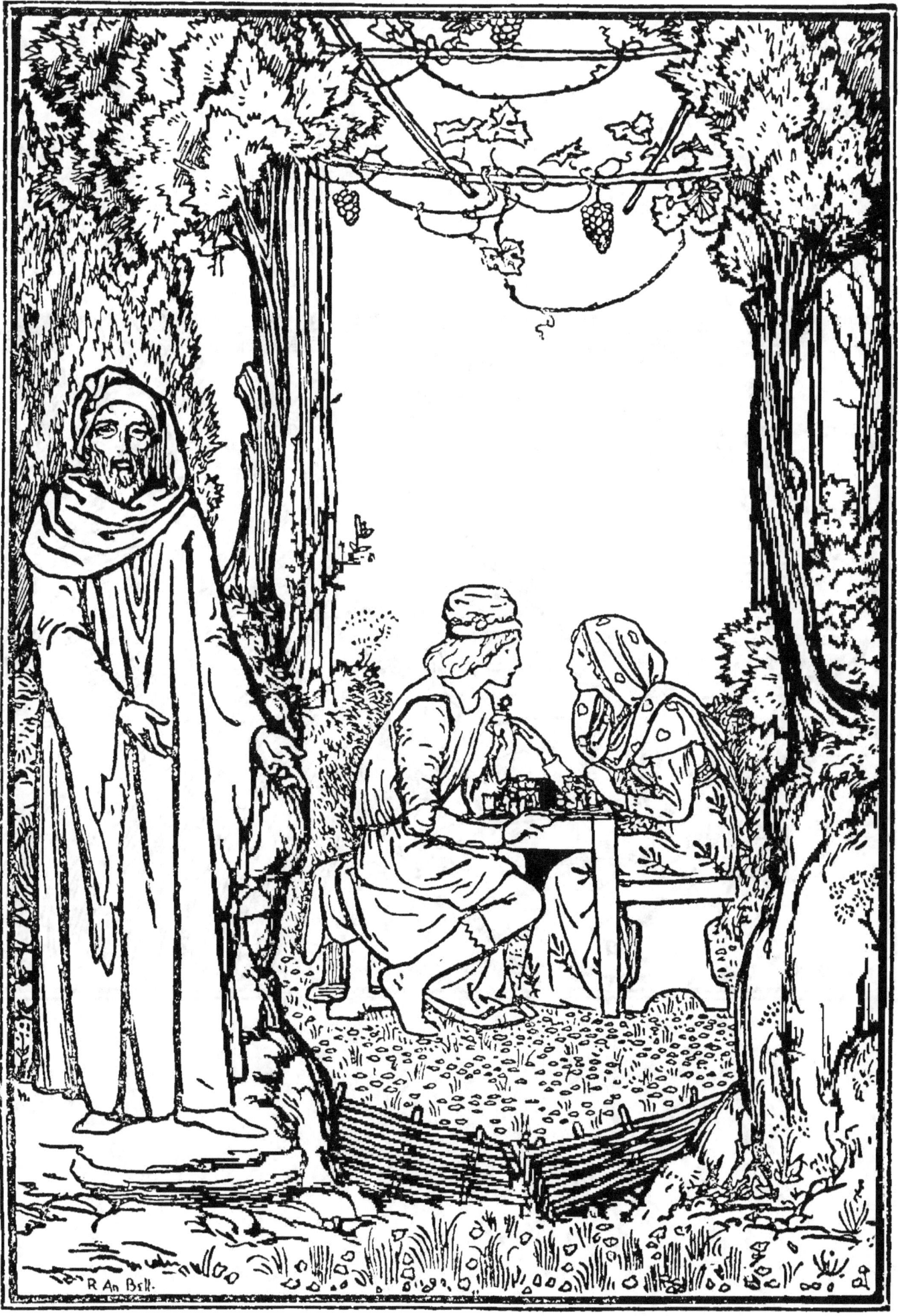

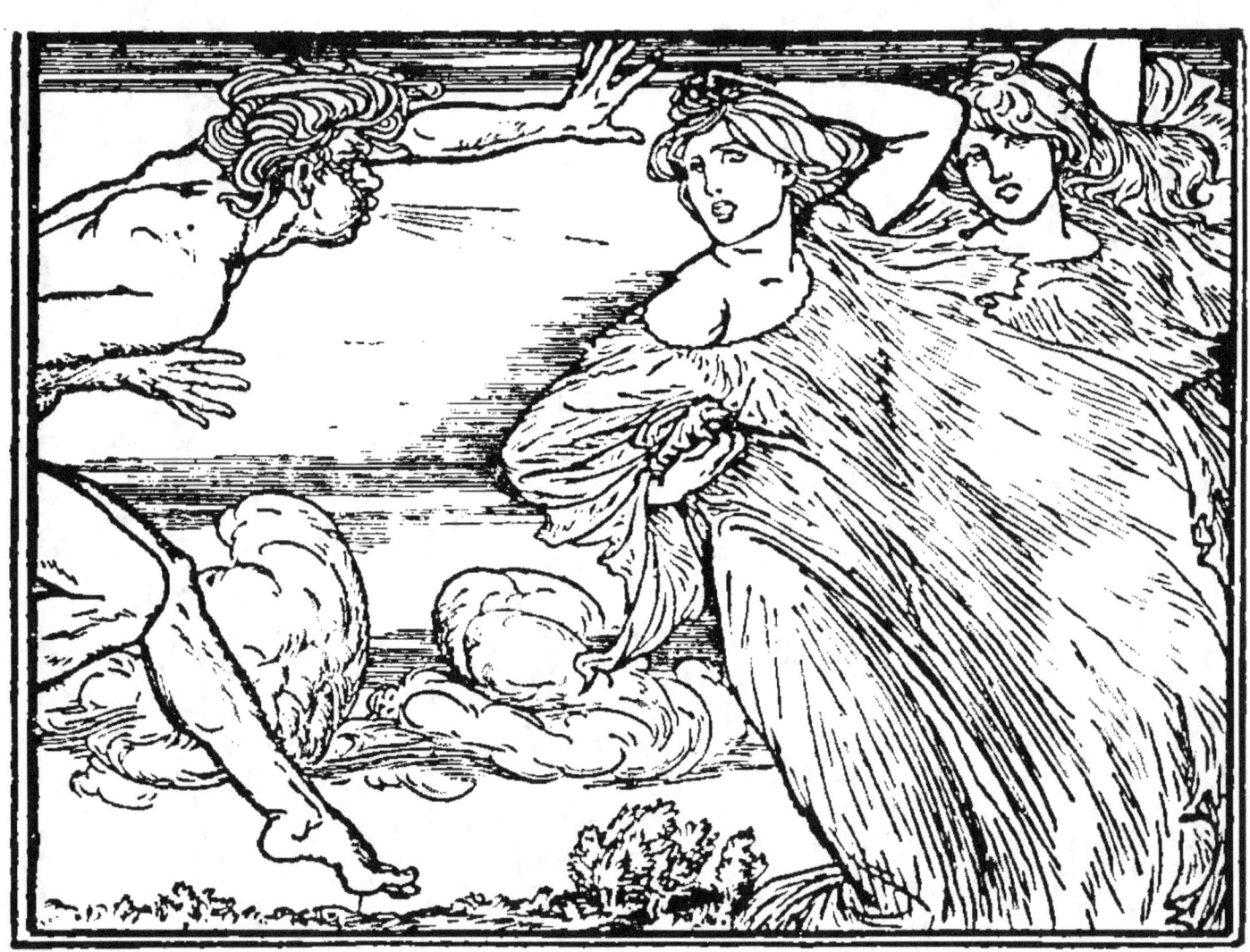

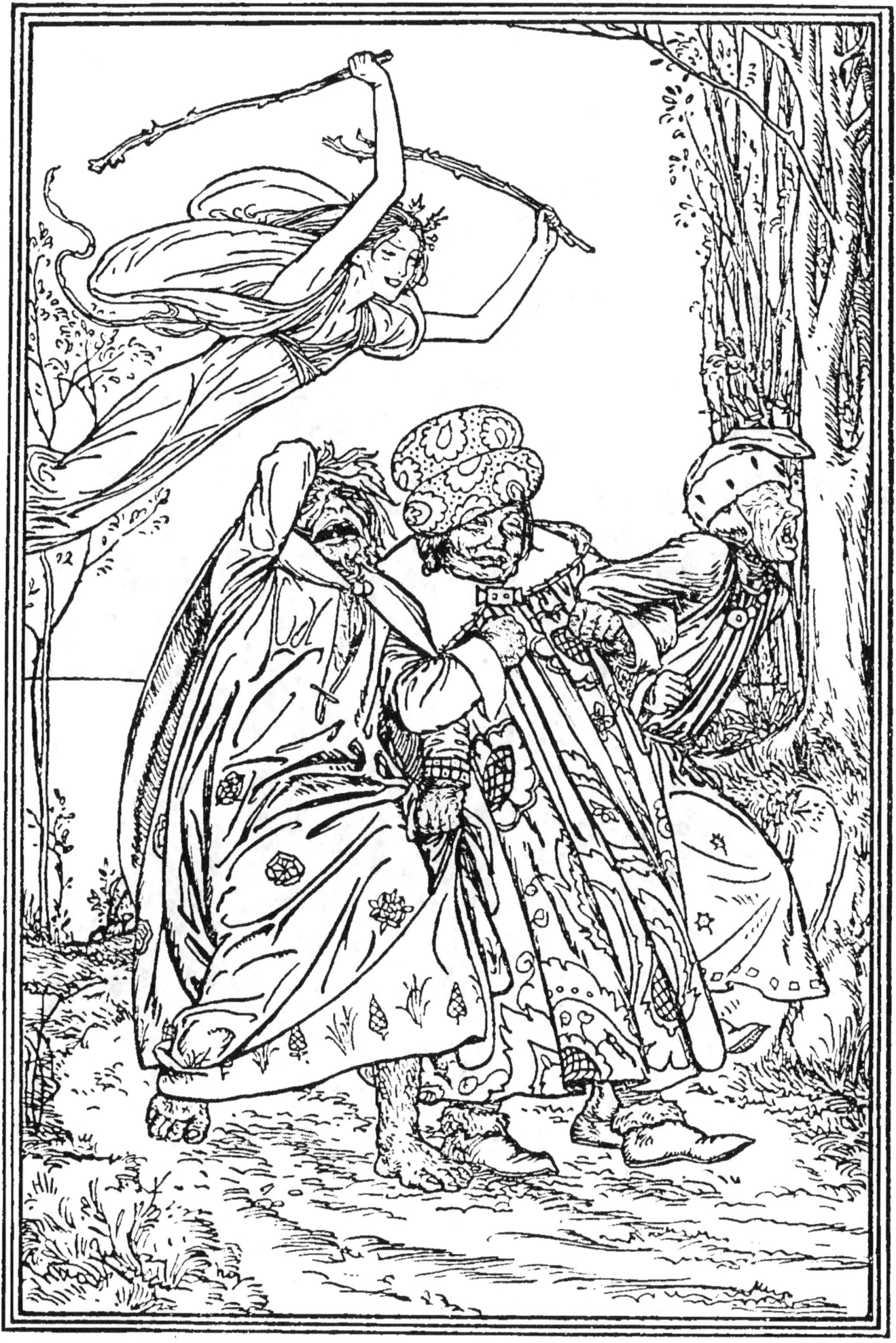

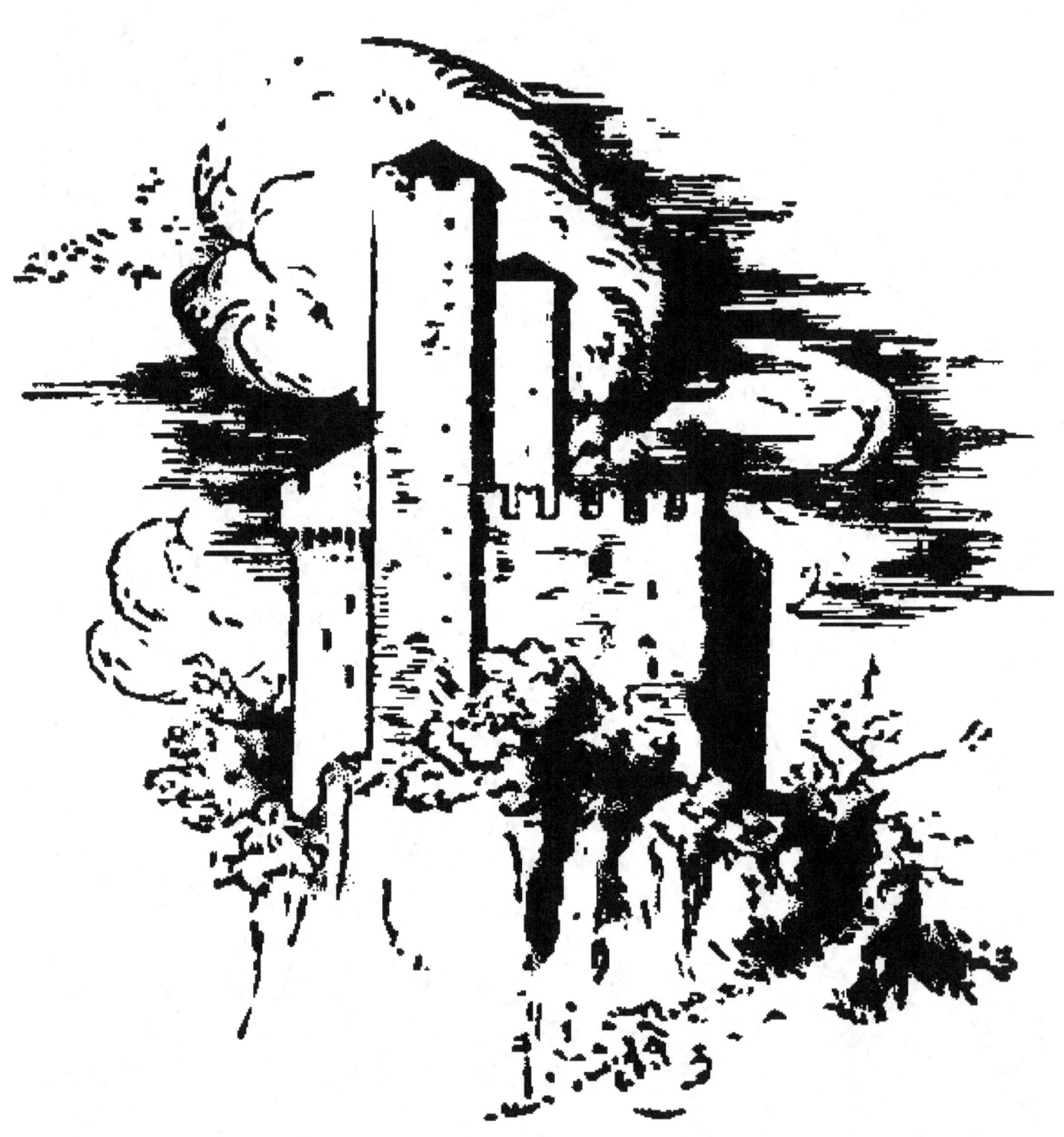

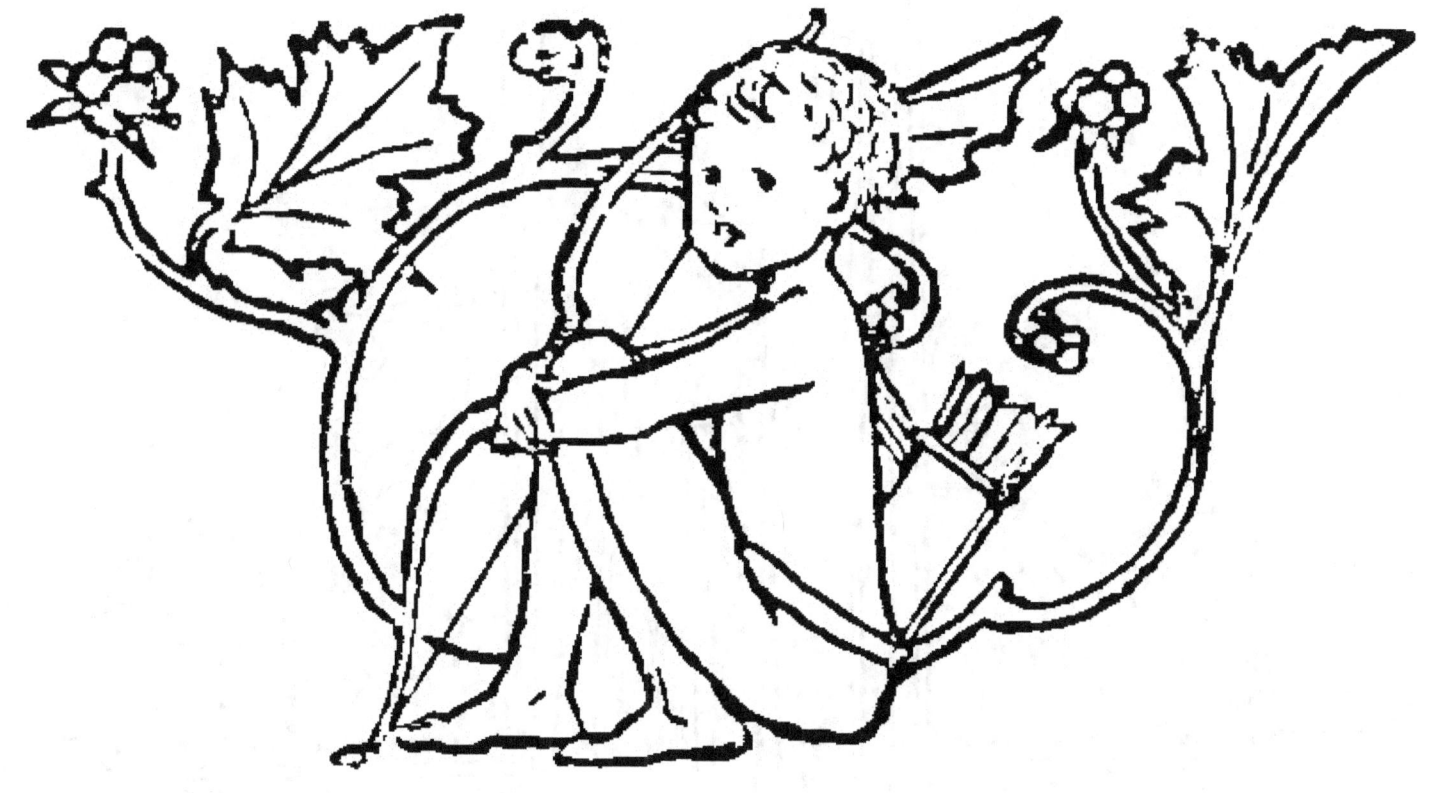

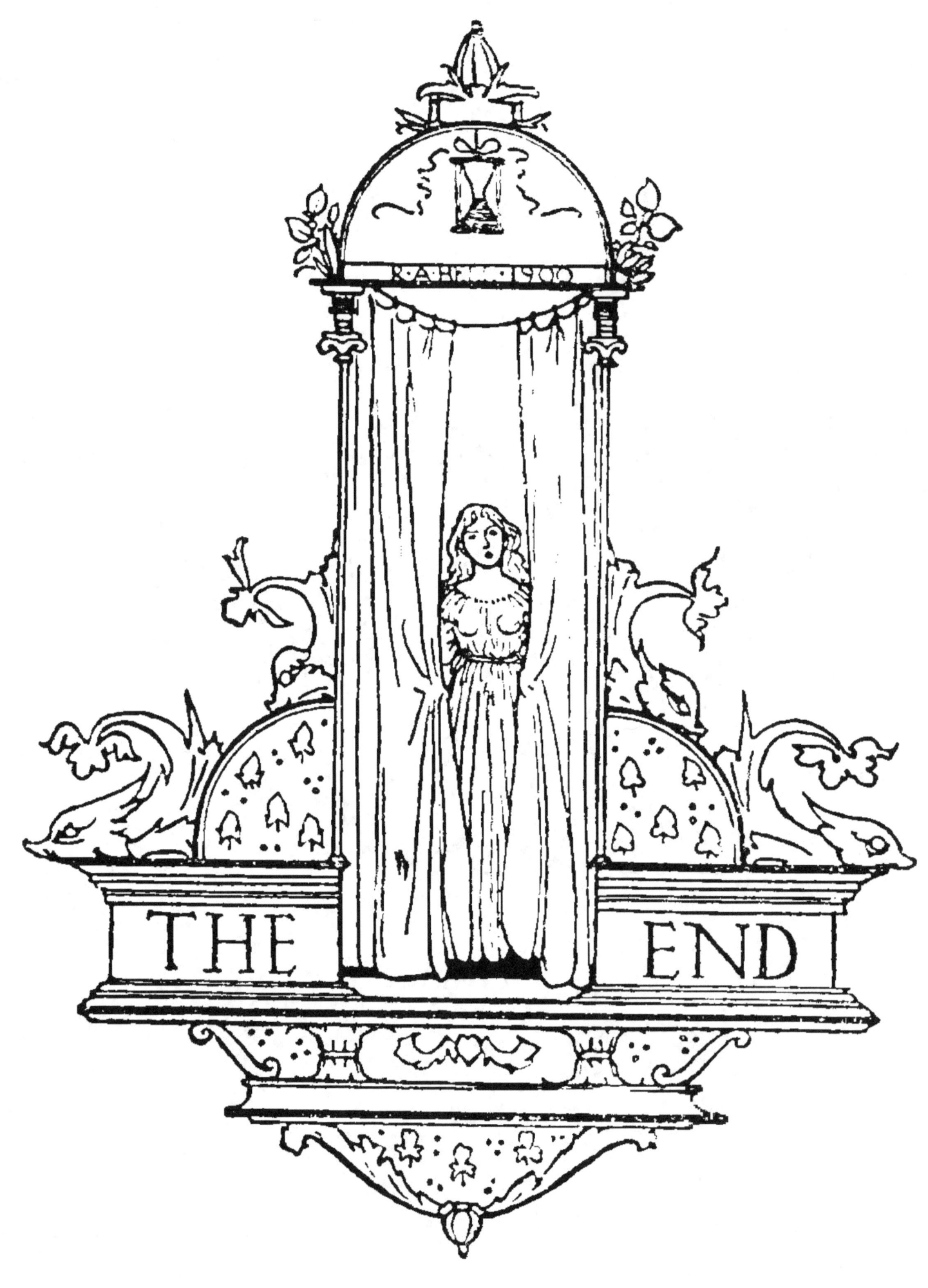

THE END

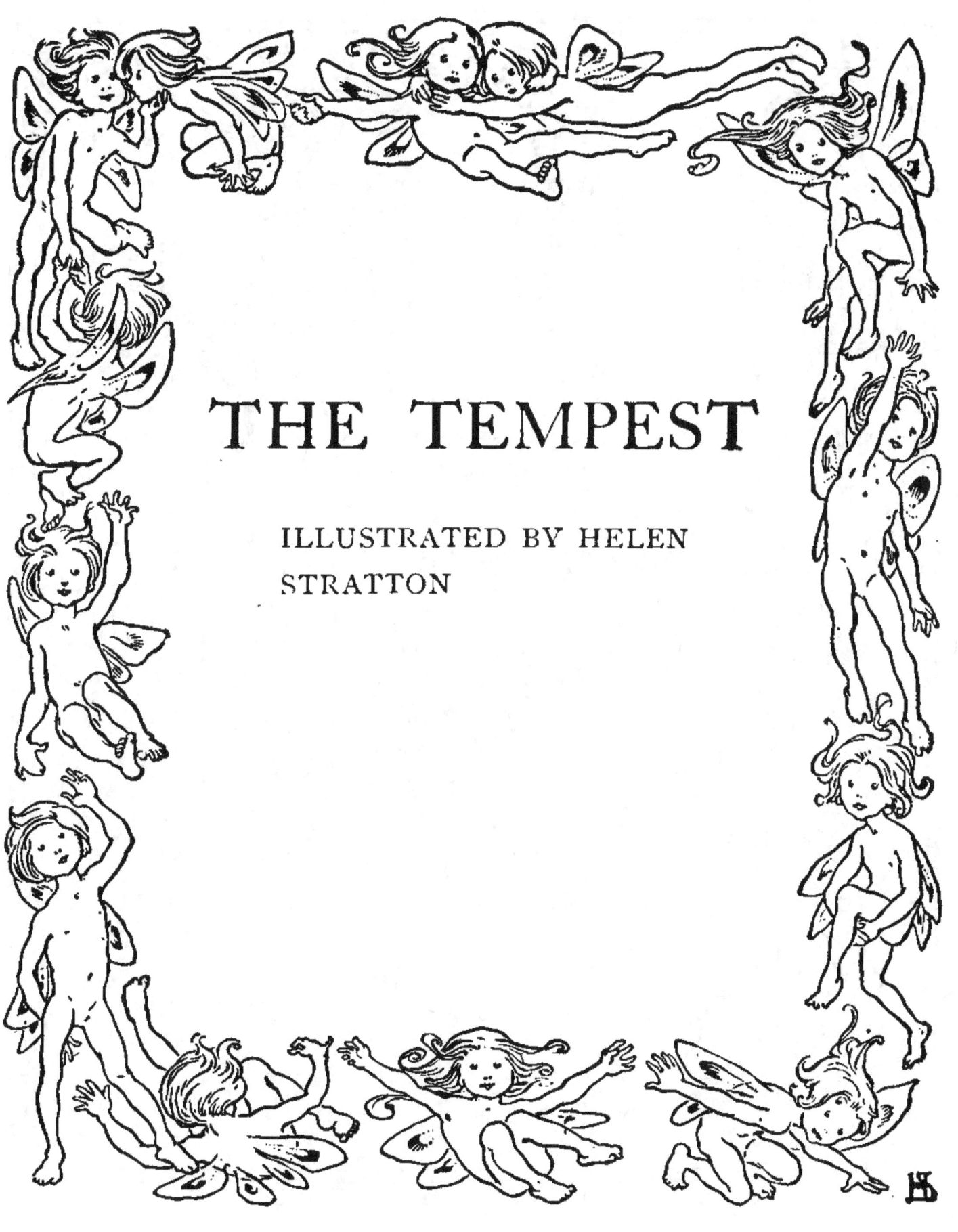

THE TEMPEST

ILLUSTRATED BY HELEN
STRATTON

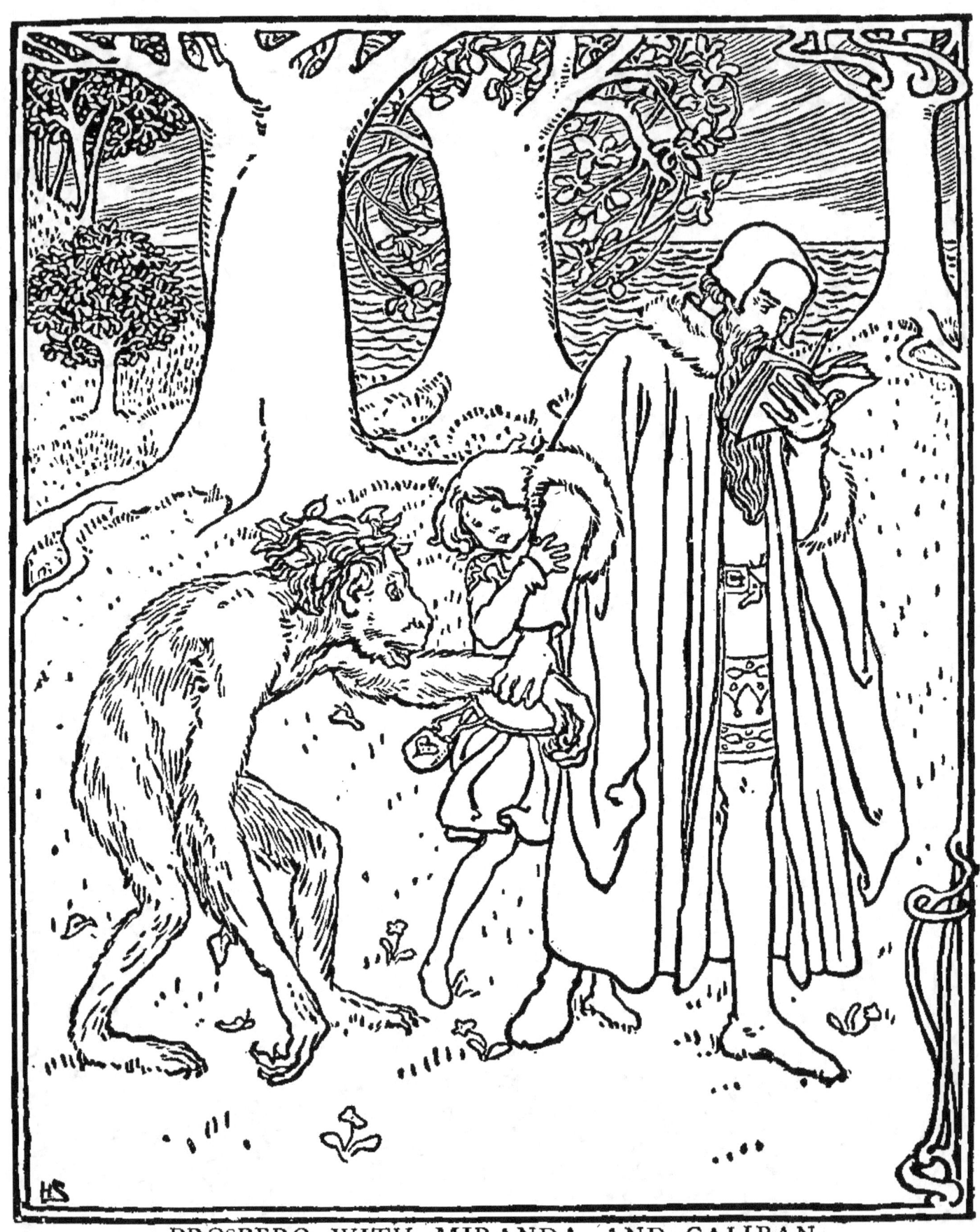

PROSPERO WITH MIRANDA AND CALIBAN

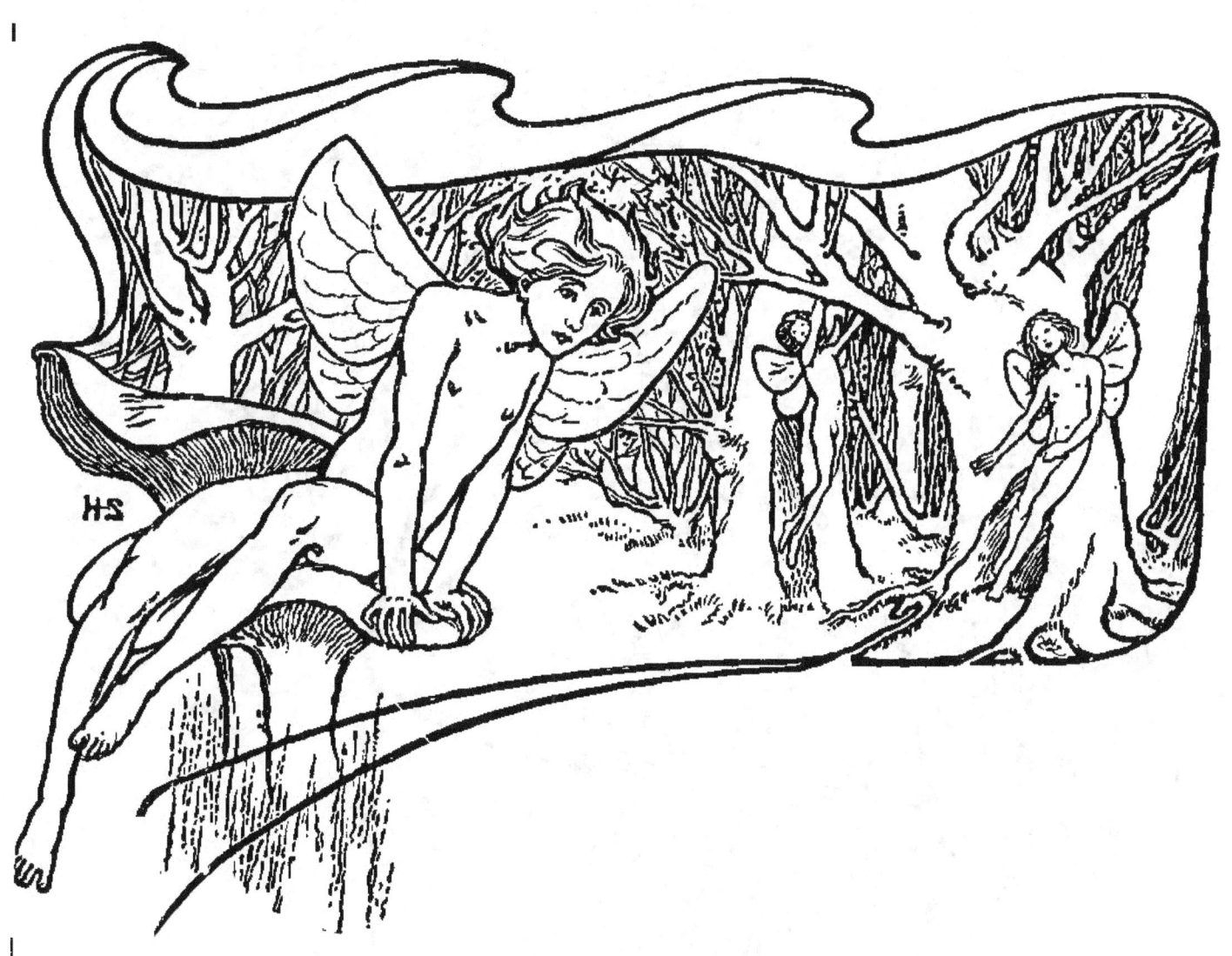

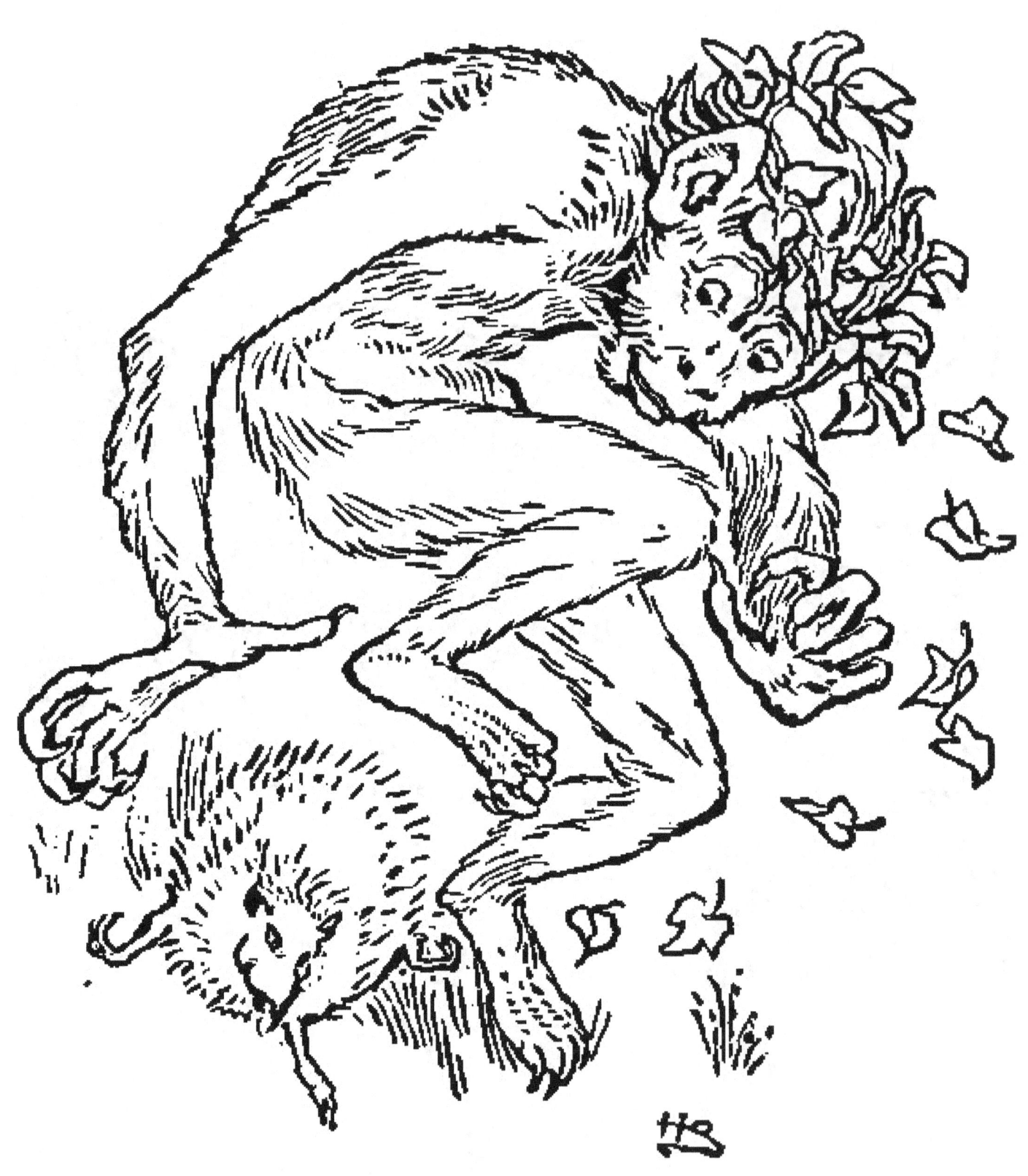

ARIEL AS A HEDGEHOG

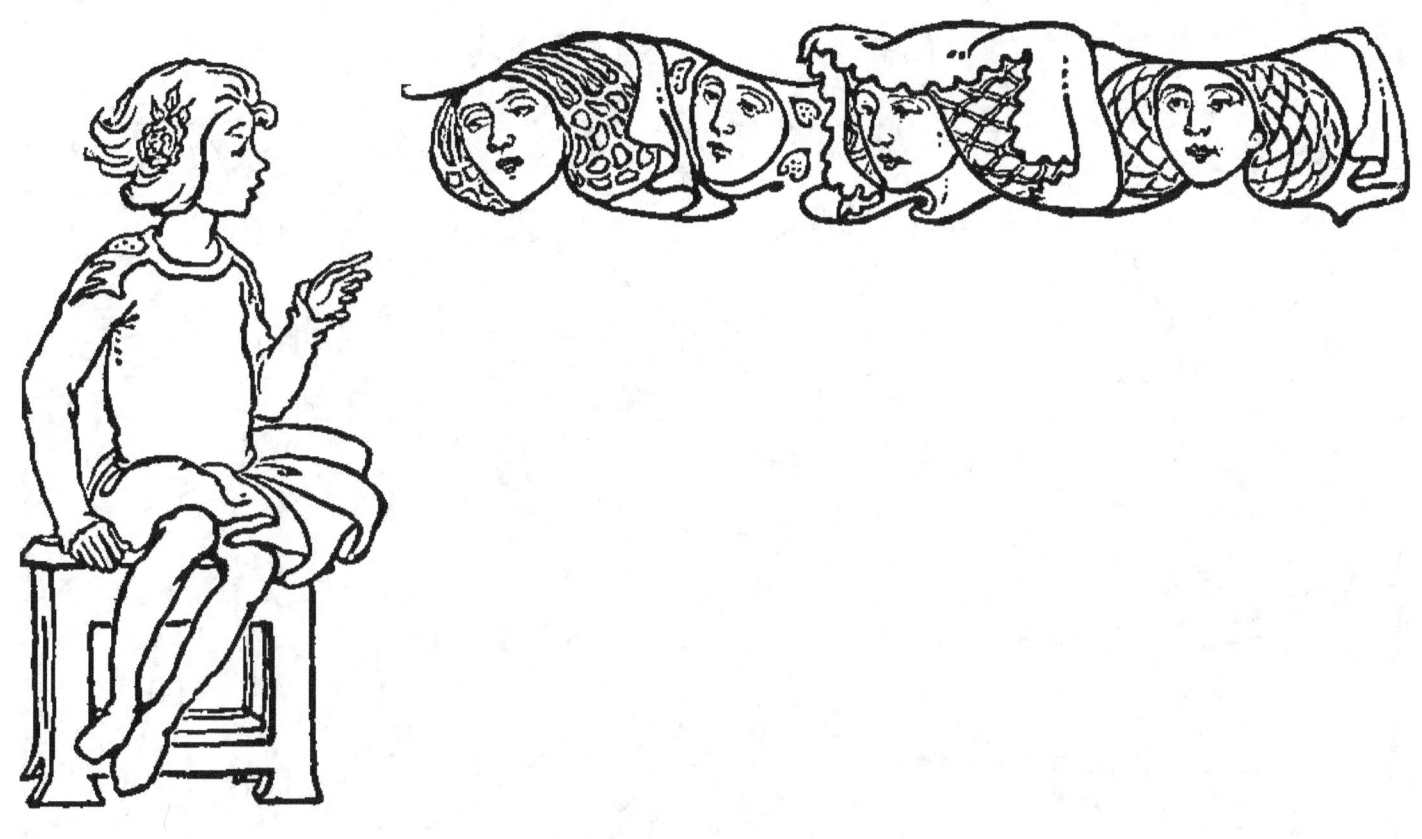

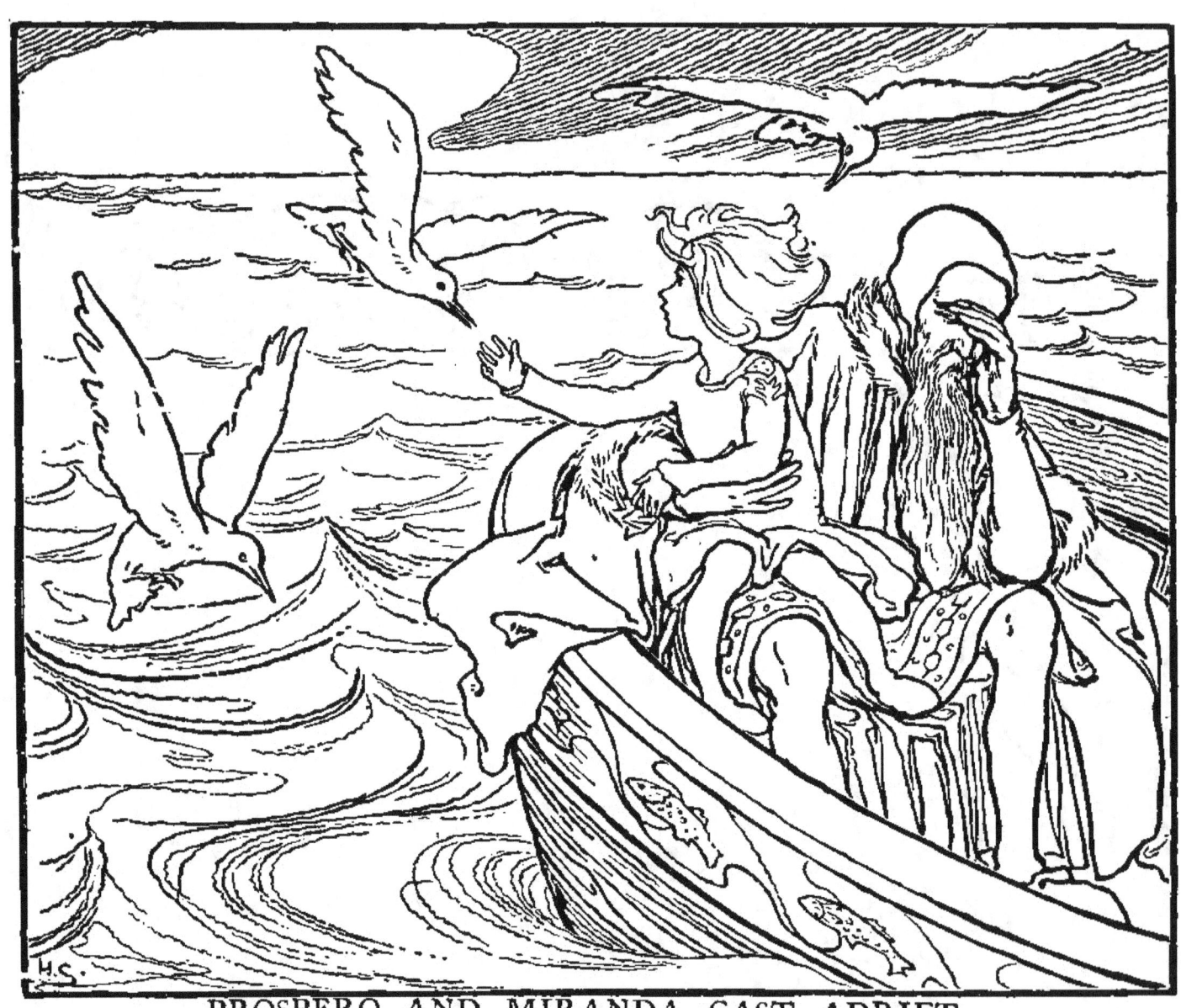

PROSPERO AND MIRANDA CAST ADRIFT

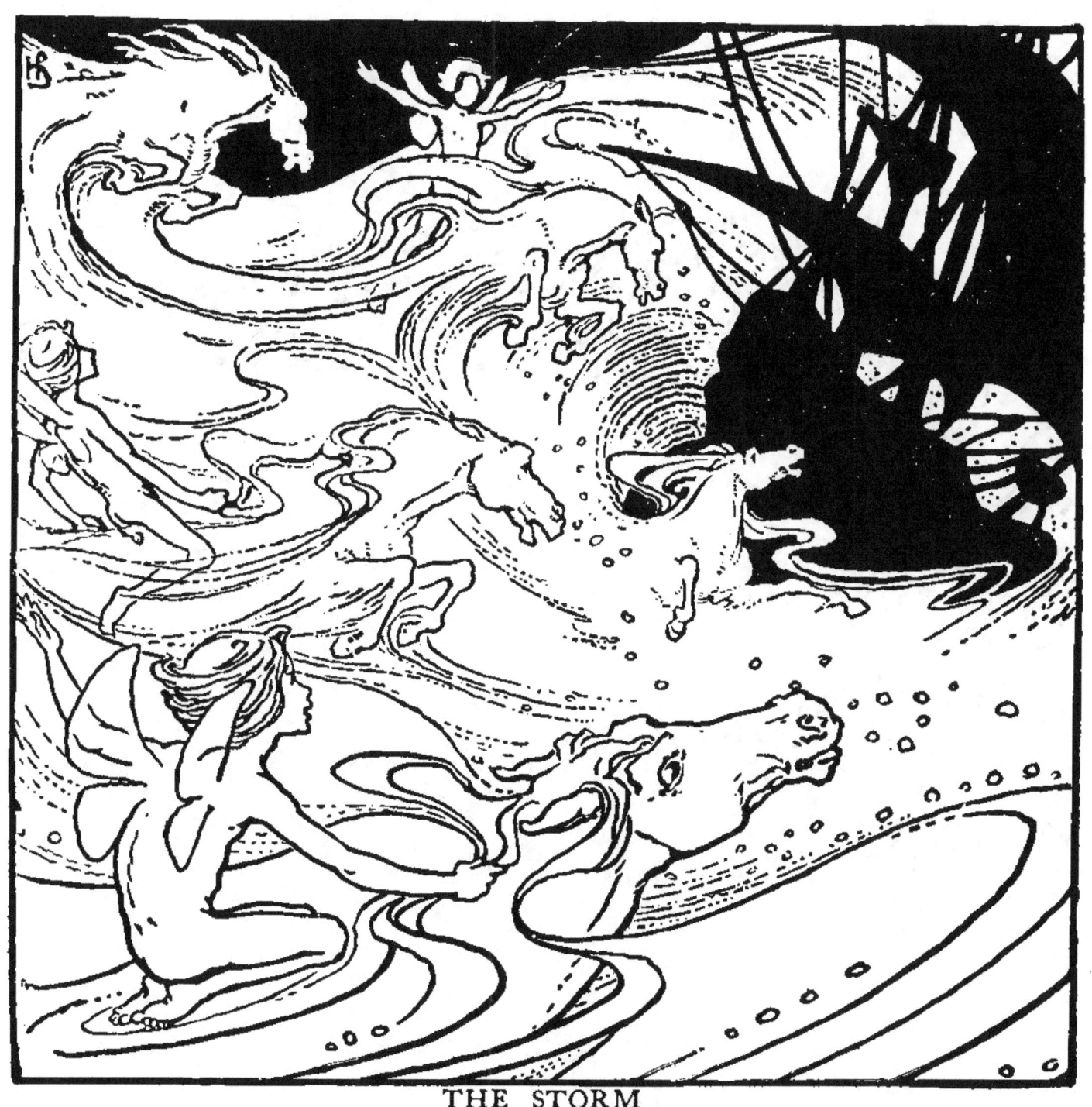

THE STORM

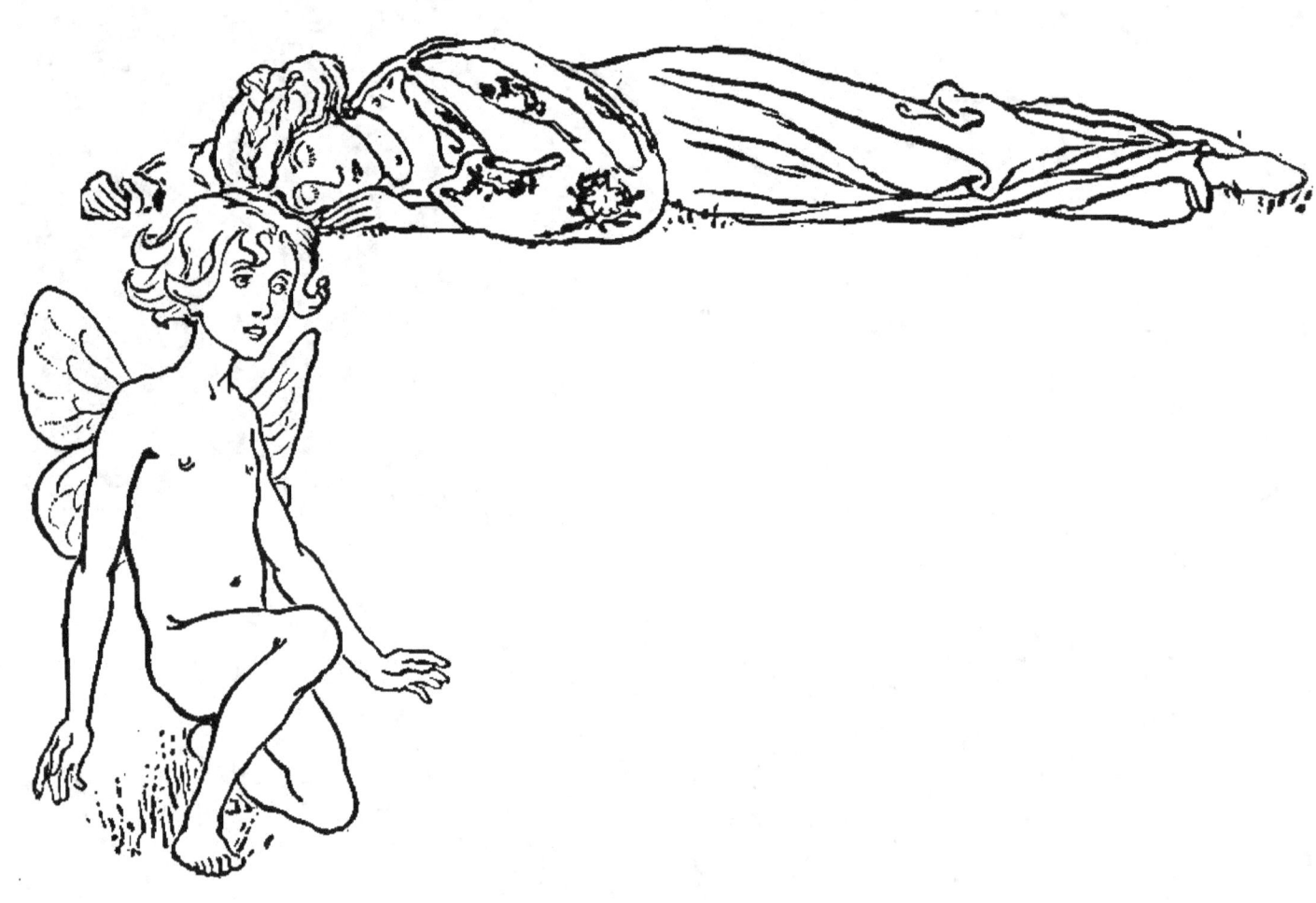

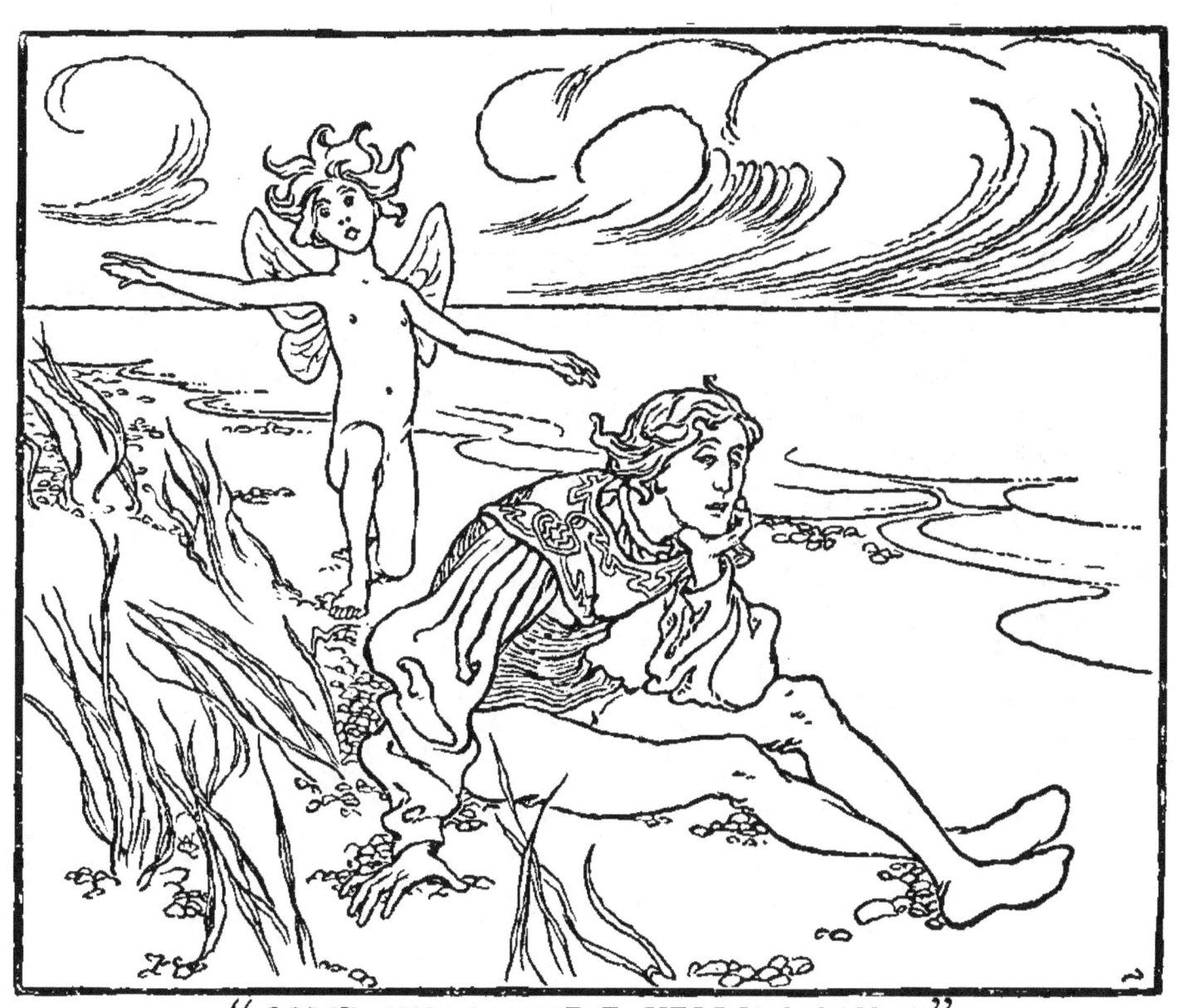

"COME UNTO THESE YELLOW SANDS"

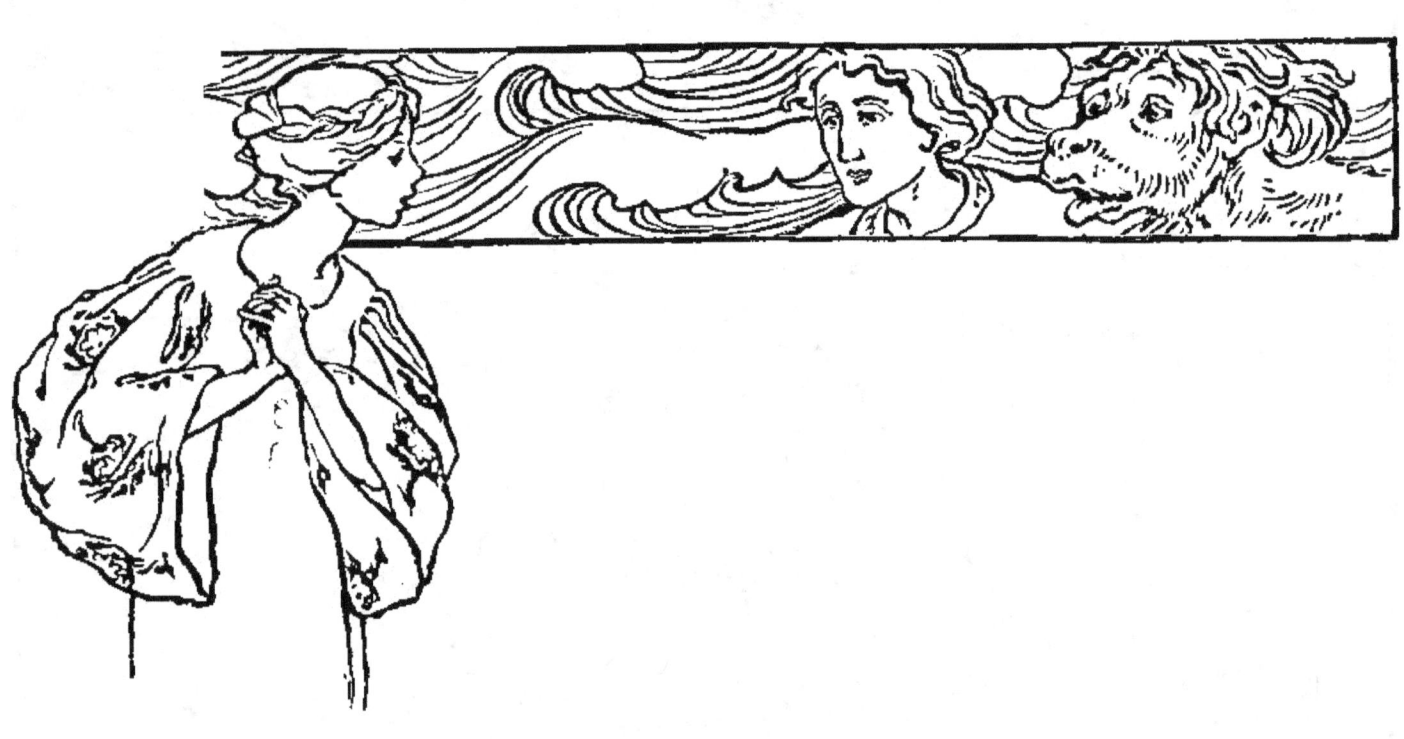

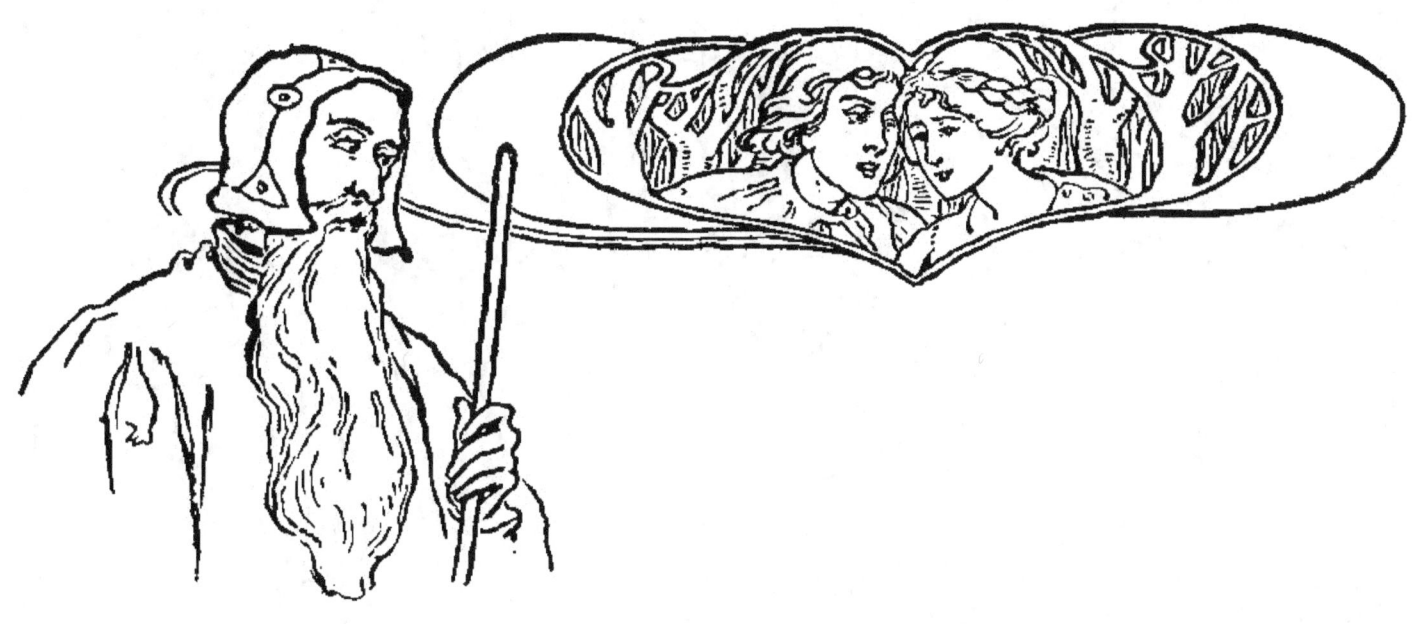

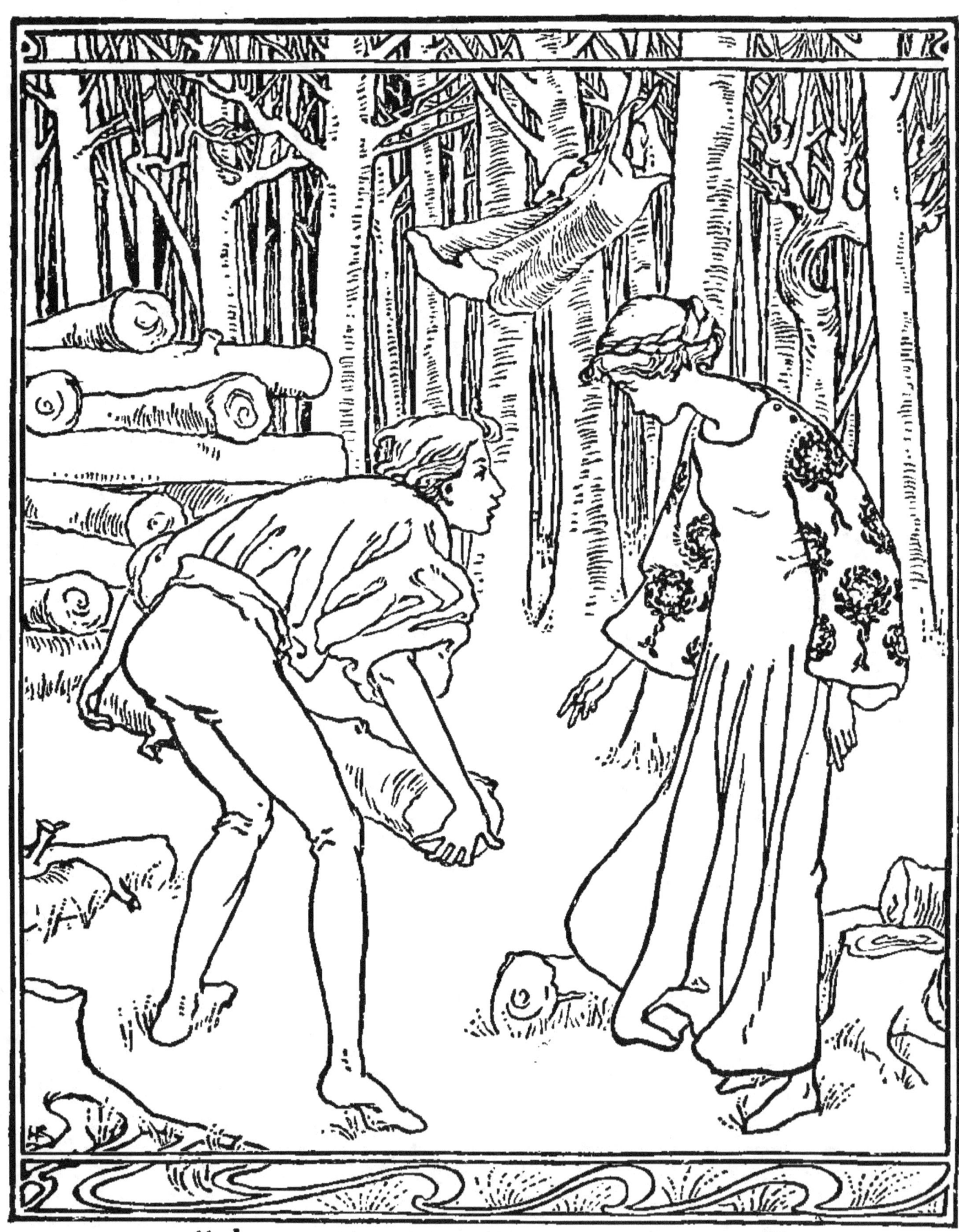

"I'LL BEAR YOUR LOGS THE WHILE"

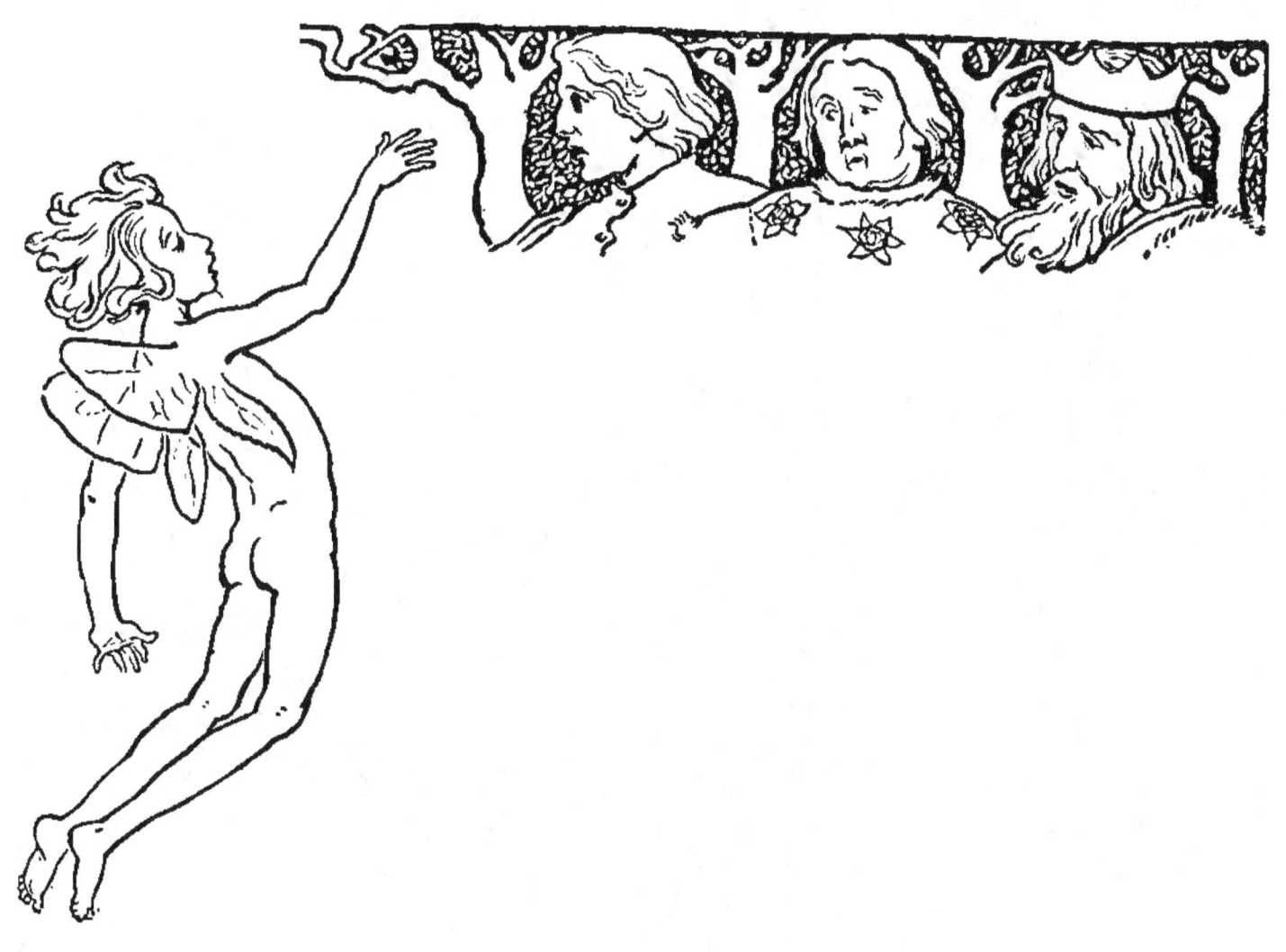

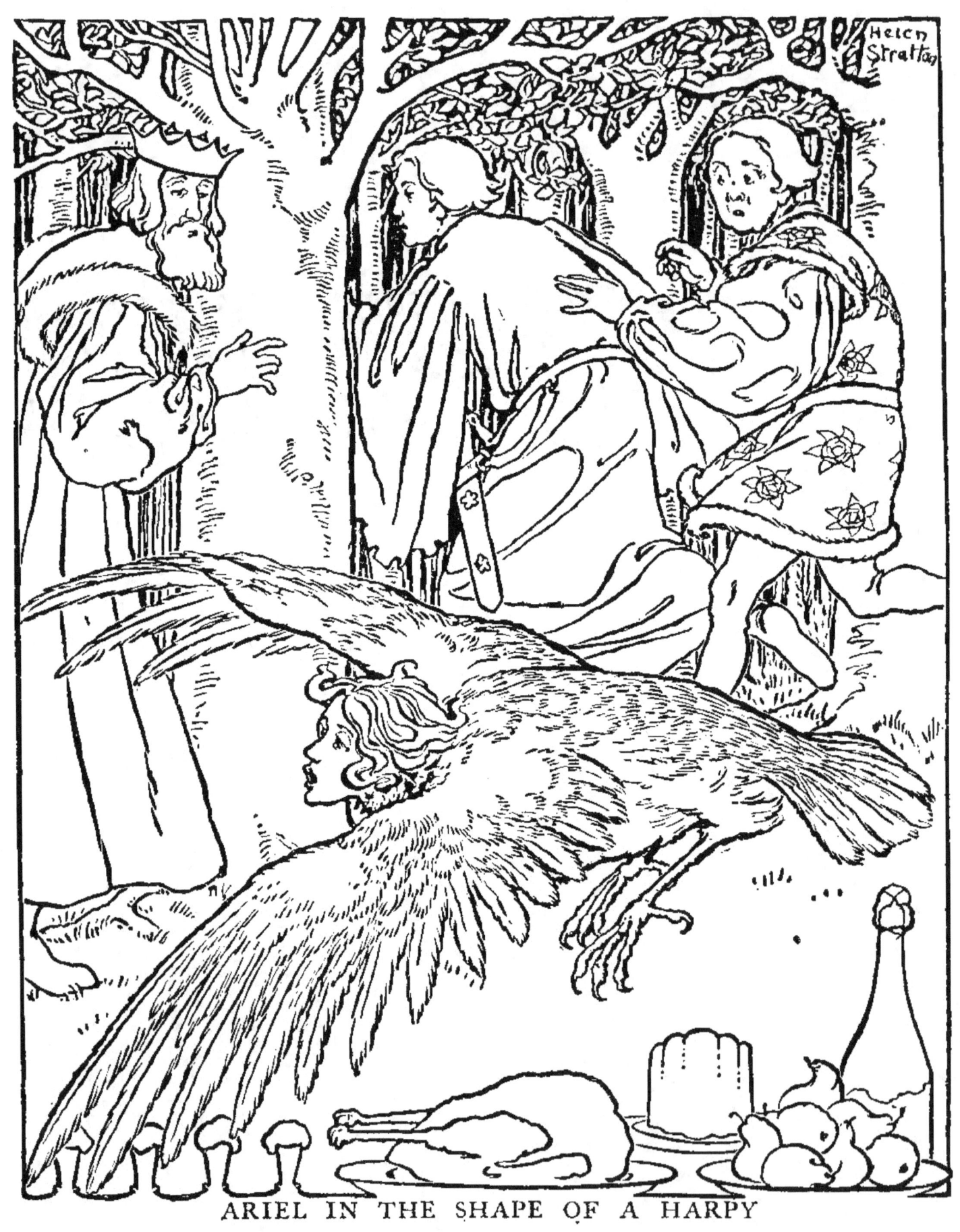

ARIEL IN THE SHAPE OF A HARPY

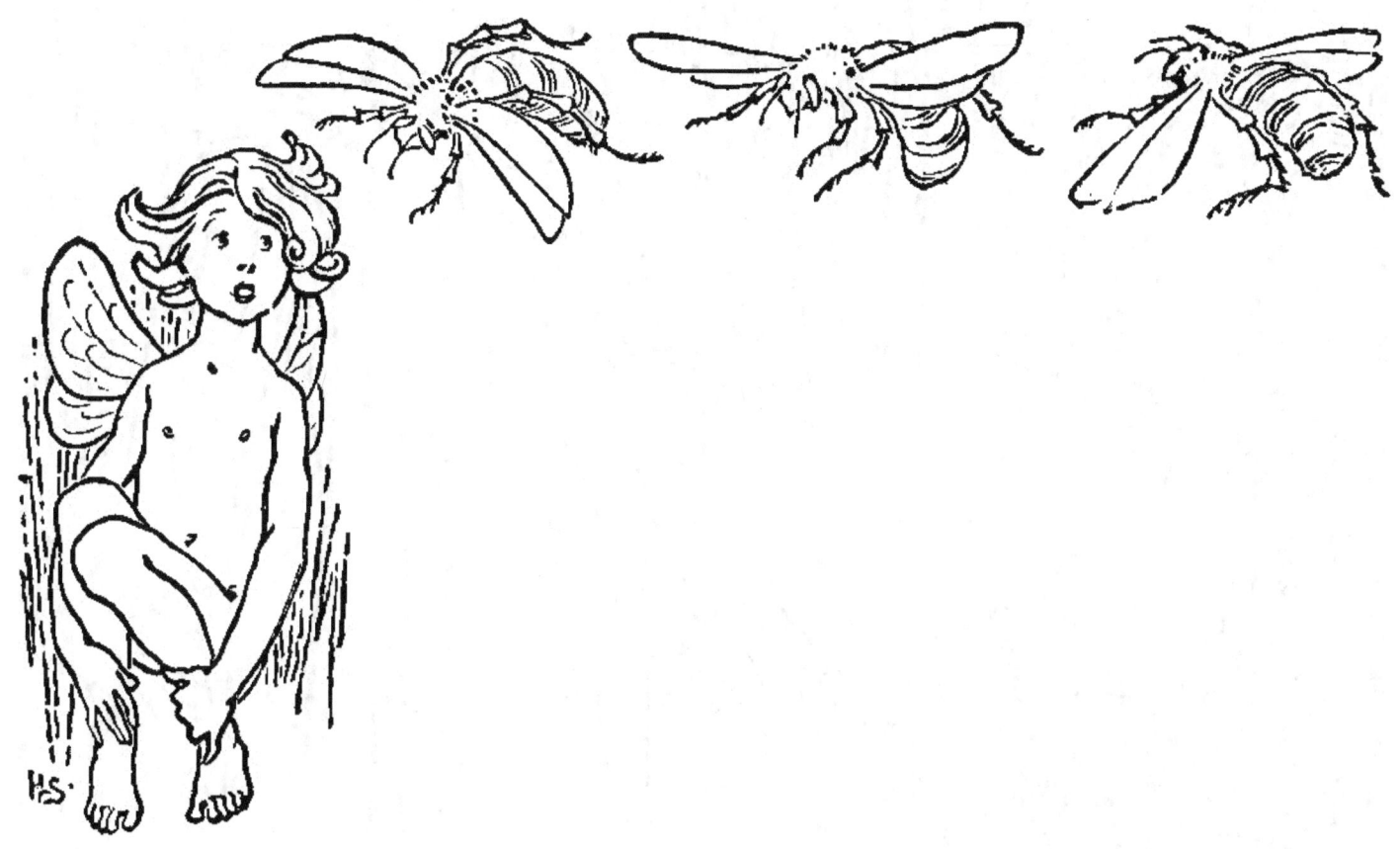

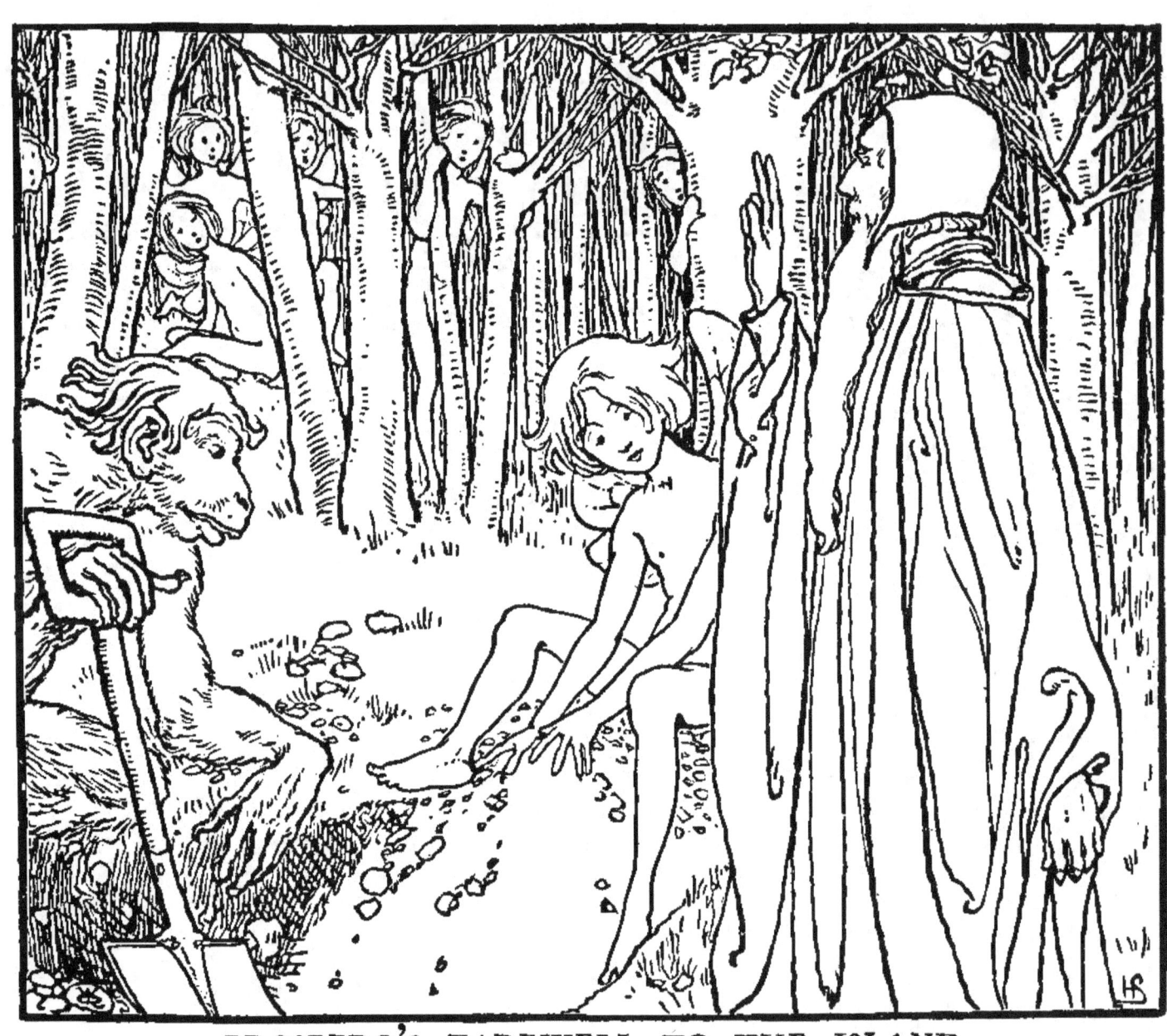

PROSPERO'S FAREWELL TO THE ISLAND

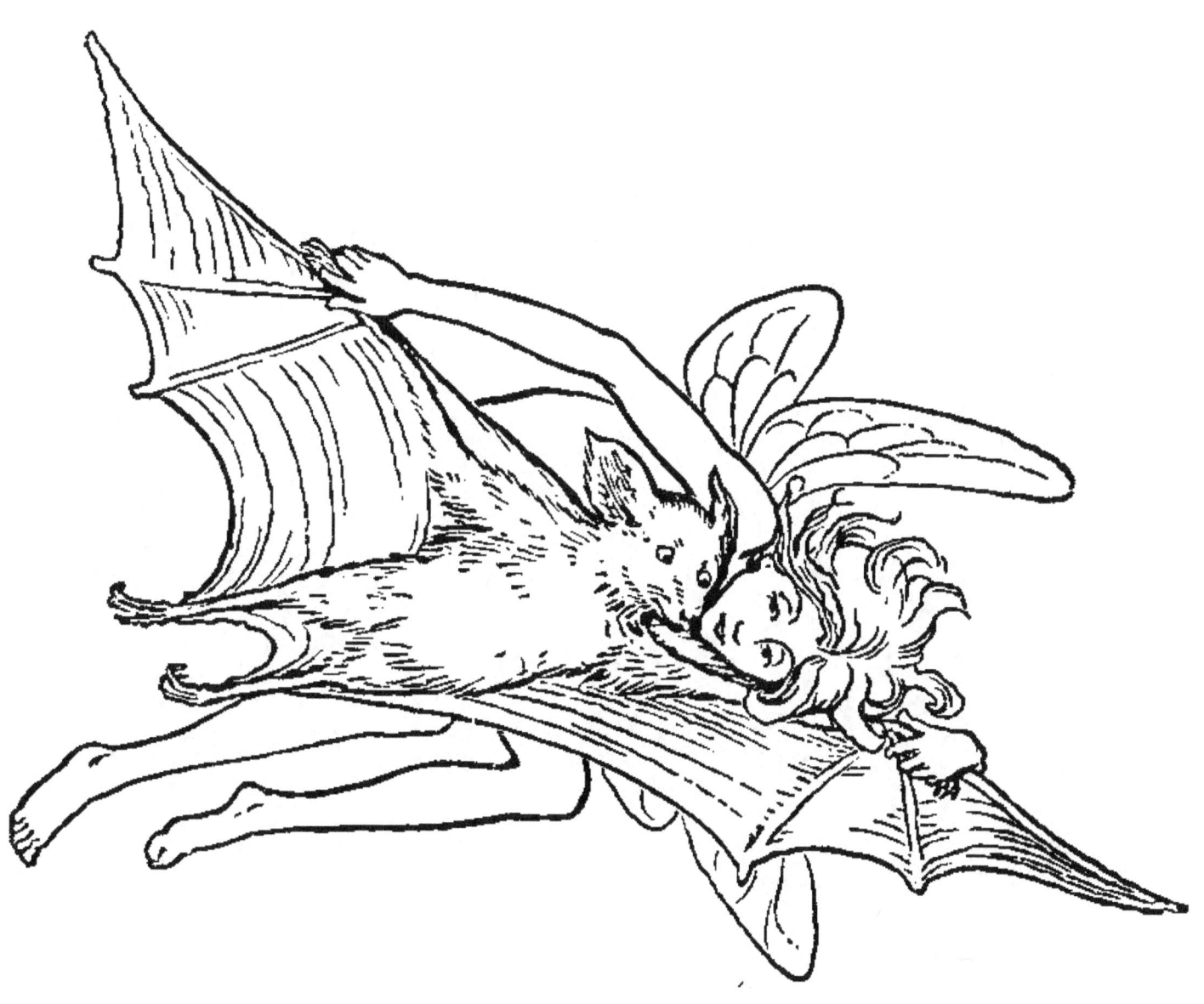